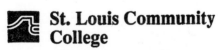

WORLD
ATLAS
of
THE PAST

THE
ANCIENT
WORLD

WORLD
ATLAS
of
THE PAST

John Haywood

THE

ANCIENT
WORLD

OXFORD UNIVERSITY PRESS
NEW YORK

Academic consultant
Dr. Paul Garwood
University of Oxford, UK

Project editor Susan Kennedy
Cartographic manager Richard Watts
Art editor & designer Ayala Kingsley

Editors Lauren Bourque, Peter Lewis
Cartographic editor Tim Williams
Picture researcher Ayala Kingsley
Picture management Claire Turner
Production director Clive Sparling
Proofreader Lynne Wycherley
Indexer Ann Barrett

AN ANDROMEDA BOOK

Produced and prepared by
Andromeda Oxford Ltd
11 – 15 The Vineyard
Abingdon
Oxfordshire, OX14 3PX
England

© 1999 Andromeda Oxford Ltd

Originated in Malaysia by Global Colour Separation
Printed in Hong Kong by C & C Offset Printing Co.Ltd.

CONTENTS

USING THIS ATLAS

This is the first of a four-volume set that charts the global story of humans from prehistoric times to the present day. The others are: *THE MEDIEVAL WORLD* (2), *THE AGE OF DISCOVERY* (3), and *MODERN TIMES* (4). Three different types of map are used in the *World Atlas of the Past*. Here are some hints on how to study the information that appears on them.

WORLD MAPS show what the world was like at a particular moment in human history. They will tell you where there were organized states and civilizations, where people lived mostly as farmers or pastoral nomads, and where they were predominantly hunter–gatherers. By following these maps through all four volumes of the Atlas you can see how human society has evolved over time and trace the rise and fall of political empires. Black circled numbers on the world maps will help you locate references on the Timeline below.

REGIONAL MAPS show the history of a particular region of the world over an extended period of time (indicated in the top right corner of the page). To help you locate historic places, modern countries and borders are shown in light gray. Hill shading is included to indicate the physical landscape.

SUPPLEMENTARY MAPS add to the information in the regional maps by illustrating a particular theme or event.

The world and regional maps have grid references (numbers running vertically down the page, letters running horizontally across it). If you want to see if a particular place is shown on a map, the index will give you the page number and grid reference (eg. 37 4D) to help you locate it.

STANDARD MAP INFORMATION

World maps

PERSIA	civilization, state, or empire
Dutch Guiana	chiefdom, dependency, or territory
Khoisan herders	tribe, people, or cultural group

Regional maps

FRANCE	state or empire
Henan	dependency, territory, or province
Goths	tribe, people, or chiefdom
ANATOLIA	geographical region
LATVIA	modern country
—— · ——	border of modern country
✗	battle
•	site, settlement, or town

INTRODUCTION

An enormous span of human history is covered in this volume, which begins more than 4 million years ago in Africa and ends at the start of the Christian era in the Middle East and Europe. During most of this time, change was incredibly slow. Our earliest human ancestors probably lived, like modern chimpanzees and baboons, in family groups. They ate plant foods and scavenged flesh from animal carcasses using simple stone tools that did not alter in the way they were made for more than a million years. Gradually humans developed larger brains and by about 100,000 years ago had evolved into the modern human species of Homo sapiens. By the end of the Ice Age, about 11,000 years ago, they had spread to almost every part of the globe. They had learned to use fire, build shelters, and hunt and kill animals with spears and other weapons, but these developments had evolved slowly, over hundreds of thousands of years.

As the climate warmed, the pace of change accelerated. Some wild foods became scarce, so people in many parts of the world began to plant wild grasses and tubers and to keep animals for meat, milk, or wool. With astonishing speed—in a little over 3,000 years—farming became established wherever soil and climatic conditions were favorable and there was a range of native plants and animals suitable for domestication.

The adoption of agriculture transformed the way human societies were organized. Crop farmers settled down to live in villages close to the fields they worked. People learned to make pottery and work metals such as copper and bronze. As distinctions in rank and wealth developed, chiefdoms emerged in many parts of the world.

The first civilizations developed in regions of great fertility, such as the Nile valley in Egypt or the Yellow River basin in China, where surplus food could be grown to feed such people as priests or craftsmen, who were not immediately involved in farming. Societies became more complex, trade helped build up wealth, and cities developed. The first writing systems were invented and people began to write down their histories and their religious myths and beliefs, giving rise to the first literature.

Wealthy, well-organized states employed great armies to coerce their less advanced neighbors. By the end of the 1st century BC, a succession of empires and states had emerged and declined in the Near and Far East, around the Mediterranean, and in parts of Central and South America.

Left *Ceremonial vessel from Crete, c.1600 BC.*

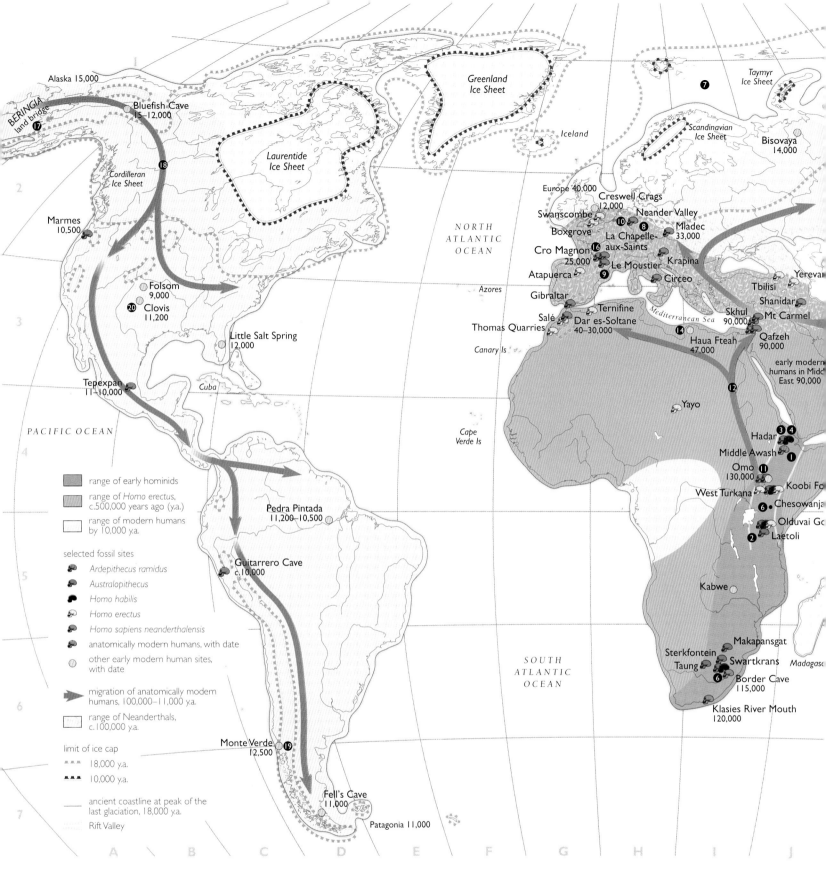

Alaska 15,000

BERINGIA land bridge ⑰

Bluefish Cave 15–12,000

⑱

Cordilleran Ice Sheet

Laurentide Ice Sheet

Greenland Ice Sheet

Iceland

Taymyr Ice Sheet

⑦

Scandinavian Ice Sheet

Bisovaya 14,000

Marmes 10,500

NORTH ATLANTIC OCEAN

Europe 40,000

Creswell Crags 12,000

Neander Valley

Swanscombe

⑩

⑧

Mladec 33,000

Folsom 9,000

Boxgrove

La Chapelle-aux-Saints

Krapina

⑳ Clovis 11,200

Cro Magnon 25,000

⑯

Le Moustier

Little Salt Spring 12,000

Atapuerca

⑨

Circeo

Yerevan

Tbilisi

Shanidar

Azores

Gibraltar

Mediterranean Sea

Skhul 90,000

Mt Carmel

Tepexpan 11–10,000

Cuba

Ternifine

Salé

Dar es-Soltane 40–30,000

Qafzeh 90,000

Thomas Quarries

Canary Is

⑭

Haua Fteah 47,000

early modern humans in Mid East 90,000

PACIFIC OCEAN

Cape Verde Is

Yayo

⑫

Hadar ③ ④

Middle Awash ①

Pedra Pintada 11,200–10,500

Omo 130,000

⑪

Koobi Fo

West Turkana

⑥ Chesowanja

Guitarrero Cave c.10,000

② Laetoli

Olduvai G

Kabwe

SOUTH ATLANTIC OCEAN

Makapansgat

Sterkfontein

Swartkrans

Madagasc

Taung

⑥

Border Cave 115,000

Monte Verde 12,500 ⑲

Fell's Cave 11,000

Klasies River Mouth 120,000

Patagonia 11,000

range of early hominids

range of *Homo erectus*, c.500,000 years ago (y.a.)

range of modern humans by 10,000 y.a.

selected fossil sites

Ardepithecus ramidus

Australopithecus

Homo habilis

Homo erectus

Homo sapiens neanderthalensis

anatomically modern humans, with date

other early modern human sites, with date

migration of anatomically modern humans, 100,000–11,000 y.a.

range of Neanderthals, c.100,000 y.a.

limit of ice cap

18,000 y.a.

10,000 y.a.

ancient coastline at peak of the last glaciation, 18,000 y.a.

Rift Valley

❶ c.4,400,000 y.a. *Ardepithecus ramidus*, the oldest human ancestor yet discovered

❷ c.3,600,000 y.a. A family of early hominids walking on two legs leave footprints in wet mud at Laetoli, Tanzania

❸ c.3,500,000 y.a. The most complete *Australopithecus afarensis* (known to her discoverers as "Lucy")

❹ c.2,400,00 y.a. Oldest known tools are in use at Hadar, Ethiopia

❺ c.1,800,000–1,600,000 y.a. *Homo erectus* migrates from Africa to reach southeast Asia

❻ c.1,600,000 y.a. First known use of fire at Chesowanja and Swartkrans in Africa

❼ c.1,000,000 y.a. Ice Age begins

❽ c.400,000 y.a. Wood tools in use in Germany

❾ c.300,000 y.a. A site at Terra Amata, France, may be evidence of the first human structure

❿ c.150,000 y.a. Neanderthals evolve in Europe

⓫ c.130,000 y.a. The earliest known modern human, *Homo sapiens sapiens*

⓬ c.100,000 y.a. Modern humans begin to migrate out of Africa

⓭ c.60,000–40,000 y.a. Australia and New Guinea reached by island-hopping sea voyages

⓮ c.47,000 y.a. Bone flute found at Haua Fteah, North Africa, is first known musical instrument

⓯ c.40,000 y.a. Australian rock carvings and cave paintings are first examples of human art

THE WORLD BY 10,000 BC

THE STORY OF HUMAN EVOLUTION BEGAN MORE THAN
5 MILLION YEARS AGO. THE FIRST REAL HUMANS
APPEARED 2.4 MILLION YEARS AGO IN EAST AFRICA.
THEY GRADUALLY BECAME SKILLED IN THE USE OF
TOOLS AND FIRE AND WERE ABLE TO ADAPT TO NEW
ENVIRONMENTS. BY 100,000 BC MODERN HUMANS HAD
BEGUN TO MIGRATE OUT OF AFRICA. BY 10,000 BC THEY
HAD SETTLED IN ALMOST EVERY PART OF THE WORLD.

According to the most widely accepted theory of evolution, human development began more than 5 million years ago during the Miocene epoch of the Earth's history (25–5 million years ago). At that time the climate was much warmer and wetter than it is today, and tropical forests grew across much of Africa, Europe, and Asia. Many species of apes lived in these forests, including one that was the ancestor of modern humans.

Toward the end of the Miocene, global temperatures began to cool, ice caps formed at the poles, and the climate grew drier. The area of tropical forests grew smaller, giving way to expanses of open woodland and grasslands. In East Africa, early hominids (the family of primates that includes modern humans and their immediate ancestors) were trapped in shrinking patches of forest. Before this, they had lived in the trees and moved on four feet when traveling over the forest floor. In order to cross wide stretches of open ground quickly and safely, some

Map labels

Berelekh 14,000
Dyukhtai Cave 18,000
Malaya Siya 34,000
Mal'ta 21,000
BERINGIA land bridge
central Asia 35,000
Teshik Tash
Zhoukoudian 25,000
Lantian
Langtandong
Yunxian
Zasaragi 50,000
Linjiang 67,000 ?
Okinawa 32,000
Tham Khuyen
Narmada
Taiwan
Ceylon
Philippine Is
Southeast Asia 75,000
Tabon 24–22,000
Niah Cave 40,000
SUNDA land bridge
Borneo
New Guinea
Sumatra
Java
Wadjak 50–25,000
Sangiran
Trinil Solo
INDIAN OCEAN
Bobangara 38,000
Solomon Islands 28,000
SAHUL land bridge
Australia and New Guinea 40,000
Devil's Lair 34,000
Lake Mungo 33,000
Kow Swamp 14,000
Bluff rockshelter 30,500
Tasmania 31,000

K L M N O P

16 c.40,000 y.a. Modern humans replace Neanderthals in western Europe

17 c.15,000 y.a. After crossing the Bering Sea "land bridge" humans reach North America

18 c.14,000 y.a. The Great Plains and South America are reached as ice sheets melt

19 c.12,500 y.a. Southern Chile is reached

20 c.9,000 y.a. Mammoth, mastodon, glyptodon, horse, camel, and 25 other American species are made extinct through overhunting

Right A family group of Australopithecenes search for edible roots. Their upright walking position allows them to keep a good lookout for animal predators in open country. At night they sleep in trees for protection.

hominids began walking on two feet, like modern humans.

These changes took place over millions of years. Fossil remains of bones provide us with evidence of our earliest ancestors. The oldest yet found, known by the scientific name of *Ardipithecus ramidus*, lived around 4.4 million years ago. They probably still inhabited the forests, living in the tree canopy as chimpanzees do, and it is unknown if they walked on two legs. A later species of hominid, *Australopithecus afarensis*, which appeared around 3.5 million years ago, was certainly able to do so.

By 3 million years ago this species had evolved into two types: "robusts" had massive teeth and jaws; "graciles," from whom modern humans are descended, had smaller teeth and jaws. Their brains were about the same size as a chimpanzee's (one-third the size of a modern human's). Like chimpanzees, they used stones and sticks as rudimentary tools. They lived on plant foods and also on the meat that they scavenged from dead animals.

THE FIRST HUMANS

The first human species evolved from the graciles around 2.4 million years ago. Its brain was about half the size of a modern human's. It has been given the name of *Homo habilis*. This simply means "handyman," because it made simple stone tools made by striking rocks together until they shattered into sharp flakes which could be used for cutting. They did not use their tools to hunt with, but to cut the meat from animals that had died naturally or been killed by predators such as lions and saber-toothed cats.

After hundreds of thousands of years *Homo habilis* gave way to a new species called *Homo erectus* ("upright man"). They were taller than modern humans, but in other respects were much like ourselves, though their brains were still much smaller. They were the first humans to live outside Africa. Between 1.8 and 1.6 million years ago they probably spread throughout tropical Asia, and after learning to use fire were also able to live in cooler areas of China and Europe. As well as giving warmth, fire was used to harden the ends of wooden tools, for cooking meat, and for protection.

Right The Rift Valley in East Africa is sometimes called the "cradle of humankind." It is the most important site for early human fossils in the world. Millions of years ago, when sudden floods occurred, soils were washed down the steep cliff sides of the valley. They covered over the bones of recently dead animals, including early humans, so preserving them from being eaten by carnivores or broken down by the weather. The Olduvai Gorge in particular has yielded unrivaled fossil evidence of our human ancestors.

Above and right Handaxes were made by carefully flaking stone or flint pebbles. These were made around 70,000 years ago, and might have been used to cut up the carcasses of animals as big as elephants.

THE ICE AGE

By now, the Earth was entering a period of climatic change, the Ice Age. In spite of its name, the climate was not cold all the time; there were frequent warm intervals, "interglacial periods," separating the cold, dry "glacial periods." The change between the two could be rapid, and animals and plants had to be able to adapt quickly—for example, by growing thicker fur or smaller leaves to prevent moisture loss—or go extinct. The way that

About 500,000 years ago *Homo erectus* began to evolve in different ways in Europe and Africa. In Europe, a species known as the Neanderthals developed. Their robust bodies and bulbous noses helped them survive the cold conditions by reducing heat loss. *Homo sapiens sapiens* ("wise man"), the first human species to resemble modern people in all anatomical respects, emerged in Africa some 130,000 years ago. As modern human populations increased, small bands slowly colonized neighboring areas, and by 100,000 years ago had migrated from Africa to the Middle East. Over the next 90,000 years their descendants spread out across most of the world. Sea levels were then much lower than today because so much of the Earth's water was frozen within glaciers and ice sheets. This allowed humans to travel easily on foot across areas of land that are now separated from each other by stretches of sea.

By 75,000 years ago modern humans had penetrated China and southeast Asia. Soon after their arrival they appear to have forced *Homo erectus* into extinction, probably because they were more skillful and resourceful hunters. Between 60,000 and 40,000 years ago they learned how to make boats or rafts and sailed to Australia and New Guinea, then a voyage of only 40 miles (64 kilometers) at its narrowest. Because of the colder climate, *Homo sapiens* was slow to migrate into Europe and central Asia. When they finally did so, around 40,000 years ago, they slowly replaced the Neanderthals already living there.

The Americas were the last continents to be reached by modern humans. By 15,000 years ago bands of hunters had penetrated as far as Alaska across a land bridge from Siberia. Great ice sheets blocked their way, making further progress impossible. When these began to melt 14,000–12,000 years ago, the Paleoindians (ancestors of the Native Americans) were able to reach the Great Plains of North America. These vast grasslands swarmed with herds of grazing animals, many species of which they hunted to extinction. The Paleoindians moved on into South America to reach Patagonia around 11,000 years ago. By this time only Antarctica and a few oceanic islands were without human inhabitants.

Homo erectus responded to these inhospitable conditions was by developing a bigger brain. This meant that greater intelligence could be applied to solving problems. By 1 million years ago the brain of *Homo erectus* was already three-quarters the size of a modern human's.

Homo erectus was a skillful toolmaker. Wooden throwing spears were used to hunt and kill wild animals, and stone handaxes to butcher them. They cleaned the skins of their prey with stone "scrapers," perhaps for clothing. They may have built simple shelters and lived in small family groups, traveling from place to place. At certain times of the year they moved their camps near to waterholes to hunt the wild animals that came there to drink, and foraged for edible plant foods such as fruits, nuts, and roots, knowing where and at what season they would be most abundant. Information of this kind would be passed on from generation to generation. The hunting–gathering way of life, as it is called, remained the way all humans lived until farming began. A few people, such as the Inuit of the Canadian Arctic and the San of the Kalahari Desert in Africa, still live like this today.

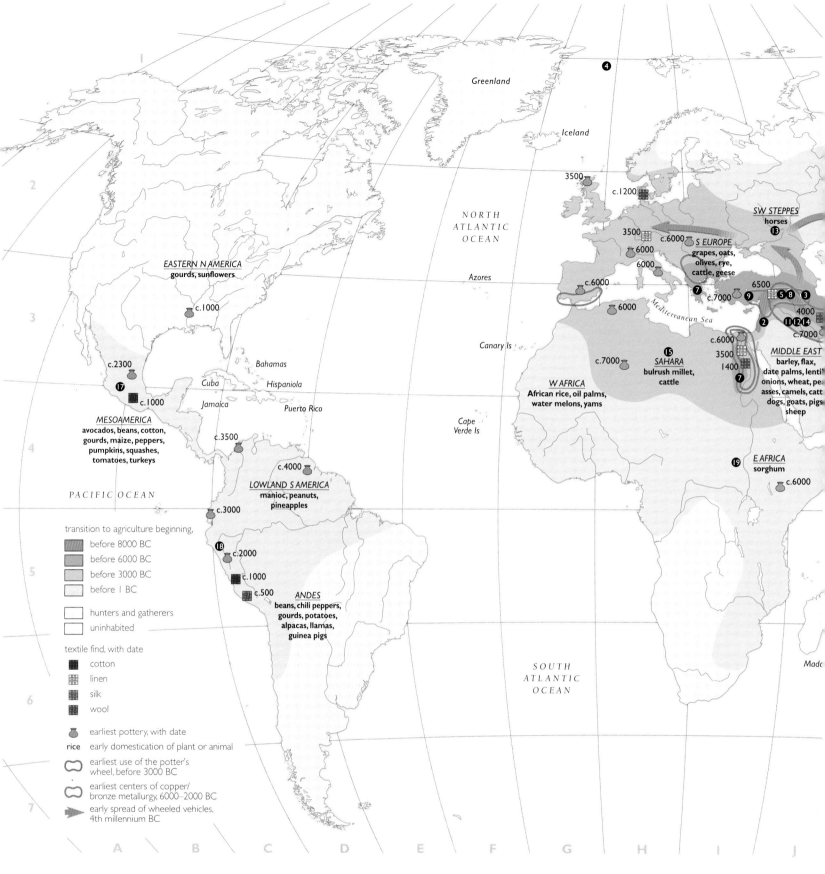

EASTERN N AMERICA
gourds, sunflowers

c.1000

c.2300

c.1000

MESOAMERICA
**avocados, beans, cotton,
gourds, maize, peppers,
pumpkins, squashes,
tomatoes, turkeys**

17

NORTH
ATLANTIC
OCEAN

Greenland

Iceland

Azores

Bahamas
Cuba   Hispaniola
Jamaica   Puerto Rico

Cape
Verde Is

PACIFIC OCEAN

c.3500

c.4000

LOWLAND S AMERICA
**manioc, peanuts,
pineapples**

c.3000

18

c.2000

c.1000

c.500

ANDES
**beans, chili peppers,
gourds, potatoes,
alpacas, llamas,
guinea pigs**

3500

c.1200

3500

c.6000

6000

6000

c.6000

6000

c.7000

SAHARA
**bulrush millet,
cattle**

15

c.6000

W AFRICA
**African rice, oil palms,
water melons, yams**

c.7000

3500
1400

7

S EUROPE
**grapes, oats,
olives, rye,
cattle, geese**

7   c.7000

6500

9

SW STEPPES
horses

13

4000

2   c.7000

11 12 14

MIDDLE EAST
**barley, flax,
date palms, lenti
onions, wheat, pe
asses, camels, catt
dogs, goats, pigs
sheep**

19   E AFRICA
sorghum

c.6000

Mediterranean Sea

SOUTH
ATLANTIC
OCEAN

Mad

transition to agriculture beginning,

before 8000 BC

before 6000 BC

before 3000 BC

before 1 BC

hunters and gatherers

uninhabited

textile find, with date

cotton

linen

silk

wool

earliest pottery, with date

rice   early domestication of plant or animal

earliest use of the potter's
wheel, before 3000 BC

earliest centers of copper/
bronze metallurgy, 6000–2000 BC

early spread of wheeled vehicles,
4th millennium BC

❶ **c.11,000 BC** The earliest known pots are made in Japan

❷ **c.10,000** Hunter–gatherers in Syria and Israel harvest wild cereals with stone sickles

❸ **c.9000** Wild sheep are domesticated by hunters in the Zagros mountains

❹ **c.8000** End of the Ice Age

❺ **c.8000–7700** Following the domestication of wheat and barley, the first farming villages develop in the Fertile Crescent

❻ **c.6500** Rice is farmed in the Yangtze valley

❼ **c.6500** Wheat, barley, sheep, and cattle farming spread to Egypt and Europe

❽ **c.6500** Wild cattle are domesticated in the Middle East

❾ **c.6200** The smelting of copper at Chatal Huyuk, Turkey, is the first known example of metalworking

❿ **c.5500** Cotton is domesticated in the northern mountains of Pakistan

⓫ **c.5000** The use of irrigation makes farming possible on the dry Mesopotamian plains

⓬ **c.4500** The plow, sail, and potter's wheel come into use in Mesopotamia

⓭ **c.4000** Horses are domesticated for meat and milk in southern Russia

⓮ **c.3800** Bronzeworking develops in the Middle East

⓯ **c.3500** Overgrazing by herds of cattle may have helped to turn the Sahara into a desert

THE WORLD BY 2000 BC

As the global climate began to warm up at the end of the Ice Age, human populations rose sharply in many parts of the world. Hunter–gatherers were forced to grow their own food as natural supplies became scarcer. Where the environment was suitable, farming began in several different places between 11,000 and 8,000 years ago. It is perhaps the most important event in human history, leading to new skills and technologies.

During the Ice Age, vast areas of the Earth were covered with grasslands grazed by huge herds of animals such as bison and reindeer. However, as it began to come to an end between 12,000 and 10,000 years ago, the climate became warmer and wetter, and the forests started to spread. Herds of large animals became scarcer, and in many places people were forced to find new sources of food, hunting small game such as deer or wild sheep, catching birds and fish, and gathering shellfish and edible plants. To ensure a reliable food supply, some people began deliberately to plant wild grasses and tubers. Others managed herds of wild animals by keeping some in pens until they were needed for food.

The next stage in the story of farming was the domestication of particular plants and animals. This was done by planting or breeding only those specimens that would produce the biggest fruits or seeds, or the best meat. Among the earliest food plants to be domesticated were the grain-bearing

Map labels

CENTRAL ASIA
camels, yaks

CHINA
millet, soybeans, rice, silkworms

INDIA
cotton, zebus

SE ASIAN ARCHIPELAGO
bananas, breadfruit, coconuts

SE ASIA
rice, taros, waterchestnuts, chickens, pigs, water buffalo

NEW GUINEA
sugar cane, sweet potatoes

INDIAN OCEAN

Taiwan
Philippine Is
Ceylon
Borneo
Celebes
New Guinea
Sumatra
Java
Timor

---

⑯ **c.3000** Silkworms are domesticated in China and the first silk cloth is made

⑰ **c.2700** Corn is domesticated in Mexico, leading to farming settlement

⑱ **c.2000** Potatoes are domesticated as a staple foodcrop in the mountains of Peru

⑲ **c.1500** Cattle herding is introduced on the grasslands of sub-Saharan Africa

⑳ **c.1200–800** Pastoral farmers on the Eurasian steppes learn to ride horseback

Right Cattle herders are depicted on this rock painting from Tassili N'Ajjer in the Sahara. It dates from c.2000 BC, when the region was still largely grassland and could support both cereal farming and herding.

cereals: wheat, barley, oats, sorghum, millet, rice, and corn. Their seeds were easy to store, usually in underground pits, until the time came for planting the next year. They are still the main food source for most of the world's people today. Herd animals like cattle, sheep, goats, pigs, camels, and horses proved the most suitable for domestication. As well as meat, they provided milk, wool, and transportation.

CRADLES OF AGRICULTURE

Farming began in a number of different places around the world, at different times, and independently of each other, between 11,000 and 8,000 years ago. Some of the earliest farmers lived in the area of the Middle East called the Fertile Crescent. This region of good soil stretches through modern Israel, Lebanon, Syria, and Iraq. The Natufian people of Syria and Israel began to grow wild wheat and barley around 10,000 BC. Around the same time, people in the Zagros mountains of Iraq, farther to the east, began to domesticate wild sheep. One reason why farming developed so early in the Middle East was that it had a rich supply of native plants that were suitable for domestication, including wild wheats, barley, pulses, and nut trees. From about 8000 BC farming villages grew up right across the Fertile Crescent. From this center, cereal farming later spread through the rest of the Middle East, Egypt, parts of sub-Saharan Africa (where native grains were domesticated), Pakistan, and Europe.

In east Asia millet and rice farming was taking place in the Yellow and Yangtze river valleys of China at least 8,000 years ago. Southeast Asia and New Guinea saw the early domestication of several tropical food crops such as taro, sugar cane, bananas, and sweet potatoes. In Mexico and South America a large range of edible plants were domesticated, including corn, beans, peppers, squashes, and potatoes. Guinea pigs, alpacas, and llamas were used for food, wool, and transportation. Several regions of the world, in particular North America, southern Africa, and Australia, had few or no native plants and animals that could be easily domesticated. Farming became important in these places only after domestic animals and crops had been introduced from other parts of the world.

FARMING & TECHNOLOGY

Farming led to new discoveries and inventions. Hunter–gatherers were nomads, so everything they owned had to be carried with them from camp to camp. Farmers, on the other hand, lived more settled lives in villages, and could keep and store more possessions. They needed more tools than before, and new implements were developed for specific purposes: polished stone axes to cut down the forests to clear fields; hoes and digging sticks to make the soil ready for planting; stone sickles to harvest crops.

New technologies arose from the need to store and prepare food. Grindstones were used to make flour from harvested grains. People began to make clay pots to store food and for cooking. The earliest known pottery comes from Japan, around 11,000 BC. It was invented independently in the Middle East around 3,000 years later. As the potters grew more skillful they learned to build ovens for baking the clay. Later, the same ovens were used to smelt and cast metals from natural ores—copper and gold first, then bronze and iron. Metal produced better cutting tools, knives, and swords.

Left A wheatfield today in Galilee, Israel. Around 12,000 years ago this area was inhabited by the Natufian people, who supported themselves by hunting gazelle and harvesting grains from wild wheat and barley. They stored these in underground pits to be used in the winter when other food was scarce. With this abundance of food always available, the Natufians began to live in settled villages. In time, they started to plant the wild cereals close to their villages so that they did not have to spend so much time traveling to find food. So the transition to farming was made.

Right Preparing food was a laborious task in early farming societies. This figurine of a woman grinding wheat comes from Egypt. Analysis of skeletal remains shows that arthritis was a common disease by age 30.

Worked metal articles were worn as jewelry, emphasizing personal wealth and status. Wheels were also developed as an aid to pottery making. Only later (around 4000 BC) was it realized that they could also be attached to carts and used to move objects. Animal skins and plant fibers had long been used for shelter, clothing, and to make baskets; now spinning and weaving developed to turn cotton, flax, and wool into cloth. This could be used to make many things, including sails for sailing ships.

There were a number of technological developments that improved the efficiency of farming. The storage and channeling of river and flood waters to irrigate fields made it possible to cultivate crops in arid regions such as the Mesopotamian floodplain, the Indus valley, and South America. When the plow came into use in central and western Europe around 3000 BC, it became easier to cultivate the region's heavy soil.

In the Eurasian steppes and sub-Saharan Africa, where there were few opportunities for crop cultivation, nomadic pastoralists managed large herds of horses, cattle, and sheep by moving them to new grazing lands once the old ones were exhausted. Around 1000 BC, Eurasian herders learned the skill of horseback riding. This made it possible for them to cover much larger distances than before.

FARMING & HEALTH

The fossil remains of hunter–gatherers show that they were taller than people are today: food supplies were plentiful and they were well nourished. This was not true of early farmers. Every few years, crops failed because of bad weather, pest invasion, or disease. During times of scarcity, malnutrition was widespread. This stunted the growth of children, and as a result early farmers were shorter than modern people. Now that they were living close to animals all the time, farmers caught many animal diseases. For example, tuberculosis, a big killer before the discovery of antibiotics in the 20th century, was originally a disease of cattle. Farmers also had to work very much harder than their hunter–gatherer ancestors and they began to develop diseases of the joints, such as arthritis.

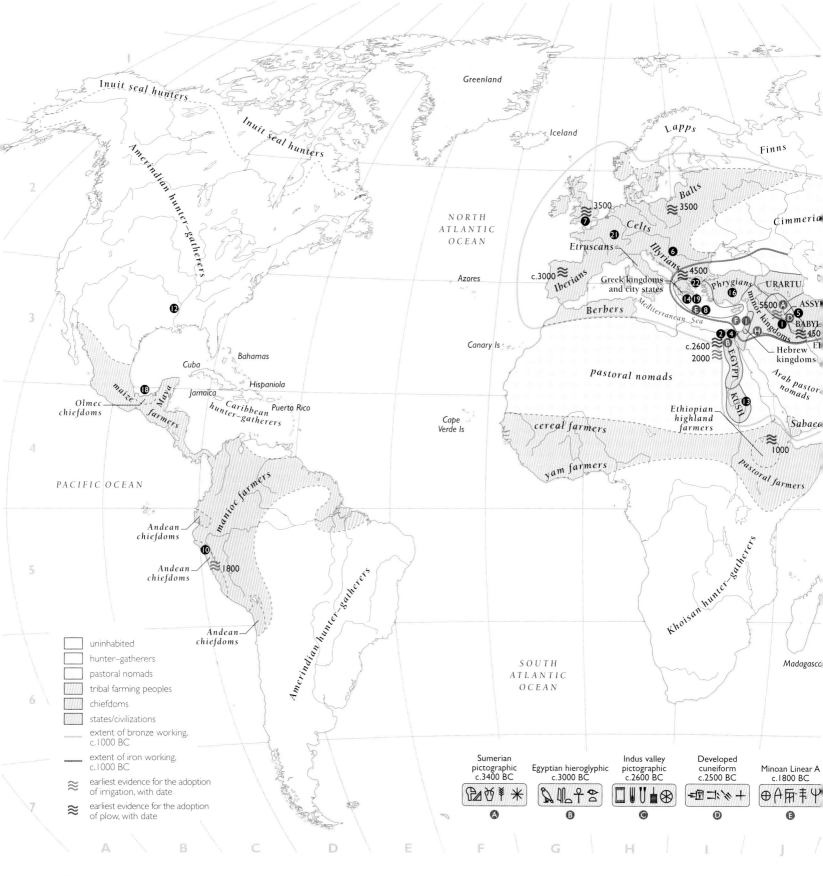

Inuit seal hunters

Greenland

Inuit seal hunters

Iceland

Lapps

Finns

Balts 3500

Cimmeria

NORTH
ATLANTIC
OCEAN

Celts

Etruscans

Illyrians

Phrygians

minor kingdoms

URARTU

ASSY

BABYL

Amerindian hunter–gatherers

Azores

c.3000

Iberians

4500

Greek kingdoms
and city states

Berbers

Mediterranean Sea

5500

450

E

Hebrew
kingdoms

Arab pastor
nomads

Canary Is

pastoral nomads

c.2600

2000

EGYPT

KUSH

Cape
Verde Is

cereal farmers

Ethiopian
highland
farmers

Sabaea

PACIFIC OCEAN

yam farmers

1000

pastoral farmers

Olmec
chiefdoms

maize

Maya
farmers

Cuba

Bahamas

Jamaica

Hispaniola

Puerto Rico

Caribbean
hunter–gatherers

manioc farmers

Andean
chiefdoms

Andean
chiefdoms

1800

Amerindian hunter–gatherers

Andean
chiefdoms

Khoisan hunter–gatherers

SOUTH
ATLANTIC
OCEAN

Madagasca

uninhabited

hunter–gatherers

pastoral nomads

tribal farming peoples

chiefdoms

states/civilizations

extent of bronze working,
c.1000 BC

extent of iron working,
c.1000 BC

earliest evidence for the adoption
of irrigation, with date

earliest evidence for the adoption
of plow, with date

Sumerian
pictographic
c.3400 BC

Egyptian hieroglyphic
c.3000 BC

Indus valley
pictographic
c.2600 BC

Developed
cuneiform
c.2500 BC

Minoan Linear A
c.1800 BC

Ⓐ   Ⓑ   Ⓒ   Ⓓ   Ⓔ

❶ c.3400 The first cities develop in Sumer (southern Iraq). At about this time a simple form of picture writing comes into use

❷ c.3000 In Egypt, writing with hieroglyphs develops and a unified kingdom is formed

❸ c.2600–1800 An urban-based civilization rises and falls in the Indus valley

❹ c.2550 The Great Pyramid is built

❺ 2334–2279 Sargon of Akkad brings all of Mesopotamia under his rule

❻ c.2500–2300 Bronze-working becomes established in central and southeast Europe

❼ c.2000 The main stage of the great stone circle at Stonehenge, southern Britain, is completed

❽ c.2000–1600 The first European civilization, the Minoan, flourishes on Crete

❾ c.1900 The first bronzes in China are made at Erlitou, which becomes a center of the craft

❿ c.1800 Large U-shaped ceremonial centers are built on the coast of Peru

⓫ c.1766–c.1122 The first Chinese dynasty, the Shang, flourishes. The first cities are built

⓬ c.1730–c.1350 In North America, hunter–gatherers build a series of complex earthworks at Poverty Point, Louisiana

⓭ c.1700 The kingdom of Kush, the first African state outside Egypt, comes into being in Nubia under Egyptian influence

⓮ c.1600–1200 The Mycenaean civilization flourishes in southern Greece

THE WORLD BY 1000 BC

WHEN FARMERS GREW MORE FOOD THAN THEY NEEDED, THEY USED THE SURPLUS AS WEALTH. AS A RESULT, DIFFERENCES OF RANK DEVELOPED BETWEEN PEOPLE AND SOCIETY GRADUALLY BECAME MORE COMPLEX. BY 1000 BC MORE THAN HALF THE WORLD'S POPULATION LIVED BY FARMING. IN SOME WELL-FAVORED PLACES, THE WORLD'S FIRST CIVILIZATIONS HAD EMERGED AND THE FIRST WRITING SYSTEMS COME INTO USE.

One consequence of the shift from hunting and gathering to farming was that human society began to change. Hunter–gatherers lived in small family groups. Most had to travel large distances to find enough food to survive—it has been estimated that an area of 10 square miles (26 sq km) of forest would yield enough food to support just one hunter–gatherer. Farmed by simple techniques, the same area of land could support 800 people. Without the need to travel to find food, people began to live in settled villages. As population figures rose, small family groups developed into larger tribes of about 1,000 people. The leaders of the tribe would meet to take collective decisions and settle disputes, but there were very few distinctions of wealth and status between individuals.

Below This massive stone head from Mexico depicts an Olmec chief or king. Early rulers had statues made of themselves to impress and intimidate their subjects, just as some dictators do in the modern world.

Map labels

Inuit
Siberian hunter–gatherers
pastoral nomads
pastoral farmers (ancestral Turko-Mongol)
Iranians
Tibetans
ZHOU c.3000
Wu
Jomon hunter–gatherers
Vedic Aryan kingdoms
Burmese
Thais
rice farmers (ancestral Vietnamese)
Dravidians
Taiwan
Ceylon
Philippine Is
Austronesians
Sumatra
Borneo
Celebes
Java
Timor
New Guinea
Papuans
INDIAN OCEAN
Lapita culture (ancestral Polynesian)
Australian Aboriginal hunter–gatherers
Tasmanian hunter–gatherers

2600
2500
3000
300

Writing systems

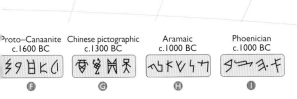

Proto–Canaanite c.1600 BC	Chinese pictographic c.1300 BC	Aramaic c.1000 BC	Phoenician c.1000 BC
F	G	H	I

L / M / N / O / P

15 **c.1500** Cattle-herding Aryans migrate from central Asia into northern India and begin to settle the Ganges plain

16 **c.1500** Iron-working develops among the Hittites in Anatolia (Turkey)

17 **c.1500–1200** The Polynesian islands (Fiji, Tonga, Samoa) are settled by people of the Lapita pottery-making culture from Melanesia

18 **c.1200** The Olmecs build elaborate ceremonial centers in Mexico

19 **c.1200–1180** The Sea Peoples bring an end to the Mycenaean civilization in Greece. They invade Anatolia and the Middle East, and are defeated by the Egyptians

20 **c.1122** The Zhou dynasty overthrows the Shang dynasty in China

21 **c.1100** The construction of hilltop forts begins in western Europe

22 **c.1000** Iron-working technology spreads to southern Europe from the Middle East

CHIEFDOMS

In some parts of the world, such as New Guinea and the Amazon basin, tribal societies like this have survived into the modern world. However, in areas where the the conditions were especially favorable for agriculture, some farmers would have been able to produce more food than they and their families needed to survive. They would have used the surplus to barter for other goods or exert power over their neighbors. Through this process, distinct inequalities of wealth and power gradually grew up between individual members of the tribe, leading to the development of chiefdoms—ranked societies of around 5,000 or more people.

Anthropologists, who study the way people live, are able to surmise how these chiefdoms were organized by looking at similar groups that have survived into the modern age; for example, in the Pacific islands. They were probably divided into extended family groups called clans. Each clan had its own hereditary leaders, and some clans had more prestige than others. The leader of the most important clan was the ruler of the chiefdom, while the leading men of the clans formed a ruling elite, or aristocracy. From the excavation of graves, archeologists can tell that differences in rank often continued after death, as some people were buried surrounded by precious objects, while others received no special treatment.

Social changes of this kind were greatest where technological improvements such as irrigation or the plow increased farming efficiency so that larger surpluses of food were produced each year. The chief and other leaders controlled the economic activity of the whole community. They did not need to work: junior members of the clan were required to give them food in exchange for leadership and protection, an early form of taxation. As the chief and other clan leaders demanded fine weapons and jewelry to show off their wealth, a small class of craftsmen developed in most chiefdoms.

The chief often had a sacred role in religious rituals and there would probably be a permanent ceremonial center, or temple, which served as a focal point for the chiefdom, with or without associated residential quarters and craft workshops. Although chiefs exploited their people, they were also responsible for organizing large building works that benefited everyone, such as the large stone monuments (megaliths) and defensive hilltop forts of western Europe or the irrigation channels of Peru.

Left The inner circle of standing stones at Stonehenge in southern England is one of the greatest monuments of prehistoric Europe. This ancient sacred site was built in several stages over hundreds of years, but the stone circle itself was completed around 2000 BC. Without the aid of wheeled vehicles or cranes, a labor force of many hundreds of people would have been used to bring the stones to the site and set them in place. They are believed to have been dragged there on sledges, some over very great distances. Only a very powerful chief could have organized such an undertaking.

great rivers: between the Tigris and Euphrates rivers in Mesopotamia (around 3400 BC); in the Nile valley in Egypt (3000 BC); in the Indus valley of Pakistan (2600 BC); and in the Yellow River basin region of China (1700 BC). In all these places, annual flood waters supported intensive farming and ensured that good harvests were had nearly every year.

Farmers brought their food surpluses as taxes to the city where they were stored in temples or palace complexes and then reissued to the people of the city who were not directly engaged in farming: bakers, potters, weavers, metalworkers, leatherworkers, and builders. As the wealth and power of the civilization increased, more classes of job were needed—soldiers to keep control and conquer new territory, traders and merchants to travel abroad and add to the city's prosperity, bureaucrats (often priests) to administer public affairs.

WRITING

By 1000 BC the major world civilizations had independently developed writing as an aid to administration. The earliest known examples of writing are accounts of goods. Found on clay tables from the city of Uruk in Mesopotamia, they date from 3300 BC. Later on, individual rulers recorded their achievements in writing on stone monuments, and the myths and stories that were central to a civilization's religious beliefs came to be written down.

Early writing systems used simple pictures as signs (pictographs). Later they developed into more complex phonetic scripts. Both systems are still used in different parts of the world today. In Mesopotamia, scribes made the pictographs by pressing a sharpened reed onto wet clay tablets, which then dried. This form of writing is called cuneiform. The Egyptians wrote on an early type of paper made from the papyrus reeds that grew beside the Nile. In China, most early writing was done on animal bones. Historians are able to decipher many, but not all, of these early scripts. Written records tell us much about past civilizations that archeology cannot do, but they still do not give us a complete picture.

THE FIRST CIVILIZATIONS

In the period c.3500–1500 BC, in several parts of the world, chiefdoms developed independently into larger, more complex civilizations, based on cities. Their populations amounted to tens of thousands, and most were ruled by kings. The king had too many subjects to rely on family or clan loyalties alone to give him authority, and his power was often based on religion. The Egyptian kings, for example, claimed that they were living gods, while the early rulers of China ruled with the support and approval of the gods. The king might also strengthen his authority by issuing laws for everyone to obey, as certain Mesopotamian rulers did.

Civilizations developed where there were rich natural resources for farming. The earliest grew up on the fertile flood plains of

Right Seals from the Indus valley marked with an unknown script. Seals like this, used by many ancient civilizations, were pressed into wet clay and used as a form of identification tag on containers, so they probably show the name of the owner. The finely carved animals may also have been a personal symbol.

ANCIENT MESOPOTAMIA

THE WORLD'S FIRST CIVILIZATION DEVELOPED IN MESOPOTAMIA MORE THAN 5,000 YEARS AGO. FOR OVER 2,000 YEARS IT WAS THE HOME OF THE WORLD'S MOST POWERFUL AND ADVANCED STATES. THE MESO-POTAMIAN CIVILIZATION HAD A STRONG INFLUENCE ON ITS NEIGHBORS IN THE MIDDLE EAST, EGYPT, AND THE INDUS VALLEY, BUT IT WAS IN DECLINE BY 500 BC AND WAS EXTINCT BY THE START OF THE CHRISTIAN ERA.

The name Mesopotamia, meaning the "land between the rivers," refers to the floodplain that lies between the Tigris and Euphrates rivers (modern Iraq). When these rivers flooded, they spread silt over the land, so creating layers of fertile soil. But very little rain falls in this region, and the land was parched and useless for farming until people learned how to irrigate it by digging canals to carry water from the rivers to their fields. This happened around 5500 BC. They were now able to cultivate the rich soils of the plains to get a reliable harvest almost every year. The invention of the wooden plow about a thousand years later, which broke up the soil prior to the seeds being sown, increased crop yields even further. The population grew, and by 4300 BC hundreds of large villages and small towns had developed in the region.

Aside from its fertile soil, Mesopotamia lacked natural resources. Wood, stone, and metal ores for every purpose from building to jewelry had to be imported from neighboring regions in exchange for surplus food and craft items such as pottery. Trade was controlled by rich and powerful rulers who organized communal projects such as the construction of irrigation canals and flood defenses. These were particularly important as floods could cause serious damage to crops and houses. They were thought to be sent by angry gods—the Biblical story of Noah's Flood has its origins in the early myths of Mesopotamia.

Left These statuettes of a man and woman praying may be actual portraits. Such figures were often placed in Sumerian temples as signs of devotion. The Sumerians worshiped hundreds of gods, and each city had its own guardian deity.

THE FIRST CITY STATES

By 3100 BC dozens of cities with populations of up to 10,000 people had emerged in Sumer, the southern part of Mesopotamia. They were independent states, each ruled by a king. Most of the inhabitants were farmers who worked in the countryside by day and returned to the city at night. The surplus crops they raised were taken to temples in the city, from where they were distributed as food rations to people not engaged in farming—those who performed specialized tasks like metalworkers, potters, builders, merchants, soldiers, and priests. Sumerian cities came to be dominated by their huge temple complexes, which acted as great storehouses for the whole community.

Early Sumerian cities were very different to modern cities. Because money had not yet come into use there were no markets. People received food, clothing, and other items as payment for work, or bartered with one another. A small number of rich people lived in palaces, but most lived in tiny houses that lacked water or sanitation. Buildings were constructions of sun-baked mud-bricks: stone was little used, except

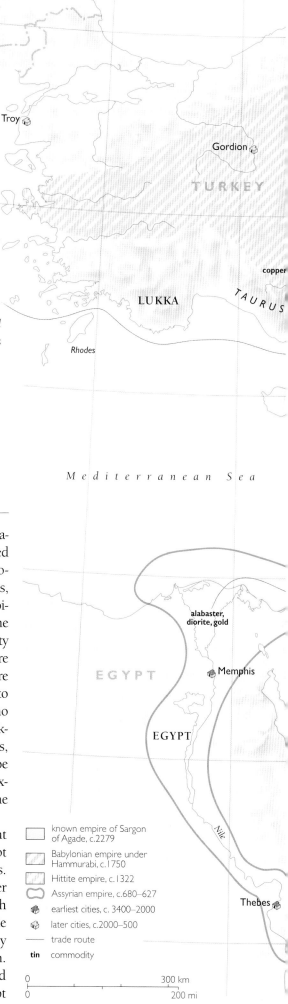

known empire of Sargon of Agade, c.2279

Babylonian empire under Hammurabi, c.1750

Hittite empire, c.1322

Assyrian empire, c.680–627

earliest cities, c. 3400–2000

later cities, c.2000–500

trade route

tin commodity

0   300 km

0   200 mi

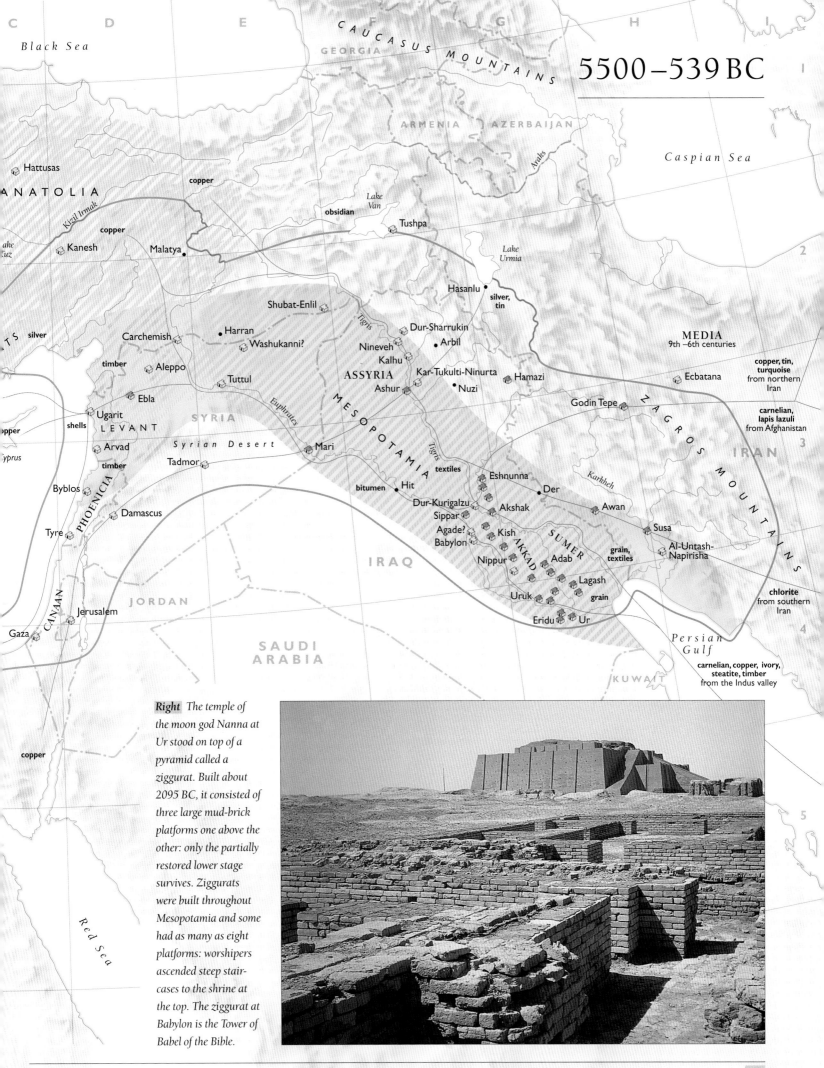

Black Sea

C D E F G H I

CAUCASUS MOUNTAINS

GEORGIA

ARMENIA AZERBAIJAN

Caspian Sea

Hattusas

ANATOLIA

Kizil Irmak

copper

copper

Kanesh

Malatya

Lake
Van

obsidian

Tushpa

Lake
Urmia

Hasanlu

silver,
tin

MEDIA
9th –6th centuries

copper, tin,
turquoise
from northern
Iran

Shubat-Enlil

Carchemish

Harran

Washukanni?

Nineveh

Kalhu

Dur-Sharrukin

Arbil

Ecbatana

ZAGROS MOUNTAINS

silver

timber

Aleppo

Tuttul

ASSYRIA

Ashur

Kar-Tukulti-Ninurta

Hamazi

Nuzi

Godin Tepe

carnelian,
lapis lazuli
from Afghanistan

IRAN

Ebla

SYRIA

Euphrates

MESOPOTAMIA

Tigris

Ugarit

LEVANT

shells

Arvad

timber

Syrian Desert

Mari

Tigris

textiles

Eshnunna

Der

Karkheh

Awan

Susa

Cyprus

Tadmor

bitumen

Hit

Dur-Kurigalzu

Akshak

Al-Untash-
Napirisha

chlorite
from southern
Iran

opper

Byblos

PHOENICIA

Damascus

Sippar

Agade?

Babylon

Kish

AKKAD

SUMER

Adab

grain,
textiles

Tyre

Nippur

Lagash

grain

CANAAN

Jerusalem

IRAQ

JORDAN

Uruk

Eridu Ur

Persian
Gulf

Gaza

SAUDI
ARABIA

KUWAIT

carnelian, copper, ivory,
steatite, timber
from the Indus valley

copper

Red Sea

Right *The temple of
the moon god Nanna at
Ur stood on top of a
pyramid called a
ziggurat. Built about
2095 BC, it consisted of
three large mud-brick
platforms one above the
other: only the partially
restored lower stage
survives. Ziggurats
were built throughout
Mesopotamia and some
had as many as eight
platforms: worshipers
ascended steep stair-
cases to the shrine at
the top. The ziggurat at
Babylon is the Tower of
Babel of the Bible.*

for sculpture, because of its scarcity. Sometimes lions came into the cities at night and prowled around on rooftops.

By around 3400 BC the Sumerians had invented a simple form of writing to record business transactions. Cuneiform writing, made by marking wet clay with a pointed reed (see page 19), slowly grew more complex over the next several hundred years. It was eventually employed for many different purposes—to record law codes and historical chronicles, send letters, and write down religious and literary texts. Because thousands of clay tablets have survived, historians have been able to piece together a remarkably full picture of the way life was led in Mesopotamian times.

During the Early Dynastic period (2900–2334 BC), disputes were common between the Sumerian city states, and most built

(see page 19)

THE ROYAL HUNT

In Mesopotamia, as in other ancient societies, hunting was a sport enjoyed by kings and men of high status. They would acquire prestige, and the approval of the gods, by displaying strength and courage in the hunting field, and it was a good training for war. The Assyrian kings were particularly addicted to the sport and decorated their palaces with scenes of their hunting prowess. Lions, then found in Mesopotamia, were considered especially worthy of being hunted by kings. Royal hunts were carefully managed. Wild animals were captured to be released in game parks for the king to pursue and kill from a light chariot.

Right *King Ashurbanipal dispatches a lion.*

sturdy walls for protection. Warfare grew more sophisticated: sculptures of the time depict warriors riding into battle in four-wheeled carts pulled by donkeys.

Around 2334 BC, Sargon, king of the city of Agade, managed to conquer all the city states of Mesopotamia and to extend his power northward as far as the Mediterranean coast. By uniting so many different peoples and cultures in a single state, he can be claimed to have created the first known empire in history. It did not long survive him, however, as rivalries once again sprang up between city states. For a time Ur, in the south, was successful, but Sumer was now in terminal decline. Power passed to the north, first to the cities of Ashur (Assyria) and Mari, then to Babylon.

HAMMURABI

Babylon reached its fullest heights in the reign of Hammurabi (1792–1750 BC). He is most famous for drawing up a list of laws, which he had inscribed on a large stone pillar, or stela. It is one of the oldest surviving legal records in the world and shows that women and children were considered to be the property of their husbands and fathers. Punishments were severe, with death or mutilation inflicted for even minor offenses.

Left *A wall panel from Nebuchadnezzar II's palace.*

TIMETABLE

c.5500
Farming develops on the floodplain of southern Mesopotamia

c.4500
The plow, wheel, and sail are in use

c.3400
The first cities grow up in Sumer

c.3300
Writing on clay tablets begins

2334
Sargon, king of Agade, establishes the world's first empire

2100
The first ziggurats are built

1813–1781
Assyria emerges as a powerful state under its king Shamshi-Adad

1792–1750
Babylon rises to power under Hammurabi

1595
Babylon is sacked by the Hittites

c.1500
Ironworking develops in the Middle East

911–627
Assyria is again the dominant power

626–612
Babylon takes over the Assyrian empire

539
Fall of the Babylonian empire to Cyrus the Great of Persia

THE ASSYRIAN EMPIRE

In 1595 BC the Hittites, who lived in the mountains of central Anatolia, where they were the first people to use iron, invaded and sacked Babylon. Soon after, Mesopotamia entered a dark age lasting 600 years. Recovery began in around 1000 BC in the Assyrian cities of Ashur and Nineveh, and by the 8th century the Assyrian empire was the dominant power in the Middle East.

Assyrian society appears to have been extremely militaristic. Even its art was concerned mostly with war. Royal palaces were adorned with carved reliefs showing scenes of battle and defeated enemies being executed, tortured, or taken into slavery. For a time Assyria even ruled Egypt, but it had dangerously overextended its power. Rebellions broke out and after the death of the tyrant Ashurbanipal (669–627 BC), the empire was seized by the Babylonians.

THE END OF BABYLON

Nebuchadnezzar II (r.604–562) was the most famous of the last kings of Babylon. He put down rebellions throughout the empire and dealt ruthlessly with his enemies: he was responsible for deporting the Jews to Babylon (see page 30). But he spent lavishly on wars and on rebuilding Babylon in imperial style (the Hanging Gardens of Babylon date from this time), and left the empire divided and impoverished.

In 539 BC Babylon fell easily to the armies of the Persian king Cyrus the Great (c.559–530). From his kingdom on the Persian Gulf, Cyrus had already conquered the vast kingdom of the Medes to the north and overrun Anatolia. He now ruled an empire stretching from the Mediterranean to Central Asia, the largest the world had yet seen. After centuries of overcultivation, Mesopotamia's soil was losing its fertility. Its neighbors overtook it in wealth and population, and under foreign rule its civilization gradually faded into oblivion.

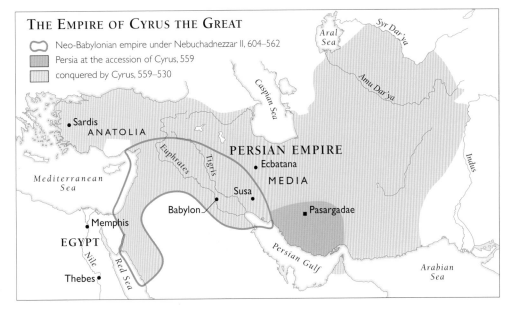

THE EMPIRE OF CYRUS THE GREAT

- Neo-Babylonian empire under Nebuchadnezzar II, 604–562
- Persia at the accession of Cyrus, 559
- conquered by Cyrus, 559–530

ANCIENT EGYPT

THE CIVILIZATION OF ANCIENT EGYPT DEPENDED COMPLETELY ON THE RIVER NILE. PREDICTABLE ANNUAL FLOODS BROUGHT THE ASSURANCE OF RICH HARVESTS YEAR AFTER YEAR, AND THE RIVER WAS THE KINGDOM'S MAIN HIGHWAY FROM NORTH TO SOUTH. TO WEST AND EAST THE DESERT PROTECTED EGYPT FROM INVASION AND WAS THE SOURCE OF BUILDING STONE AND PRECIOUS METALS. EGYPTIAN ART AND SCULPTURE VARIED LITTLE IN STYLE FOR MORE THAN 3,000 YEARS, REFLECTING THE COUNTRY'S POLITICAL AND CULTURAL STABILITY UNDER THE RULE OF THE PHARAOHS.

textiles, olive oil, wine, pottery, timber from Crete and Greece

to Cyrenaica

The valley of the Nile is 500 miles (800 kilometers) long, measured from the First Cataract, the rapids that marked Ancient Egypt's southern border, to the Mediterranean Sea. Until it broadens out into the delta, the valley is never more than a few miles wide. Sometimes it narrows to as little as a few hundred yards. On either side is desert. But despite the lack of rain, the Nile valley was one of the most favorable places for farming in the ancient world.

The river Nile rises far to the south of Egypt, in the East African highlands. Heavy rains falling here in early summer swell the river, and late in the summer the Egyptian Nile overflows its banks. When the floods retreat in the fall they leave the fields moist and covered with fresh silt. The Egyptians did not need to build flood defenses, or complex canals to irrigate their fields. They planted their seeds each autumn in the damp fertile soil left by the floods, and the crops grew through the warm Egyptian winter and were ready for harvesting in the spring, before the next flood. Only if the Nile failed to flood, as sometimes happened, did the people of Egypt go hungry.

EARLY CIVILIZATION

Farming began in the Nile valley after 6000 BC. The climate of North Africa was wetter then than it is today, and farming was even possible in the Sahara, then an area of grassland dotted with large lakes. Around 4000 BC, however, the climate became much drier and the Sahara turned to desert. Some farmers became nomadic herders, while others migrated into the Nile valley, which was soon densely populated.

A little while before 3000 BC a kingdom emerged in southern, or Upper, Egypt. The ancient Egyptian system of writing, using a form of pictographs known as hieroglyphs (see page 19), had come into use by this time. Traditionally the first king of Egypt is Narmer, who is said to have won a victory over Lower Egypt, uniting the two halves of the country. He established a royal capital at Memphis, strategically placed between the two. In the reigns of the kings that came after him, Egypt developed a strong system of government. The power of the king derived from the belief that he was the son of the sun god Ra and thought to be immortal.

From surviving records, historians have been able to compile detailed lists of the dynasties of kings who ruled Egypt, with approximate dates of their reigns. These stretch from 2920 to 30 BC, with only a few gaps. Historians divide the history of Egypt into distinct periods. The Early Dynastic period (2920–2649 BC) was followed by the Old Kingdom (2649–2134 BC), when the power of the monarchy increased and Egyptian influence extended southward up the Nile into the region then known as Nubia. Then came a troubled period when Egypt was divided between rival dynasties, (the First Intermediate Period, 2134–2040 BC). It was unified once again during the Middle Kingdom (2040–c.1640 BC).

THE PYRAMID BUILDERS

The most famous monuments of ancient Egypt, the pyramids, were built by the rulers of the Old and Middle Kingdoms as magnificent royal tombs. Their flared shape represented the downward slanting rays of the sun, along which the deceased king would ascend to heaven. These massive stone structures took many years to build and were completed before a king's death. When he died, his body was mummified: natural chemicals were used to preserve it artificially, and it was wrapped in bandages. Amulets (charms) were inserted between each layer of wrapping, and the mummy was placed inside one or more coffins. This

timber, dyes, ivory, copper, tin, glass, lapis lazuli from Lebanon and Cyprus

B

C

to the Middle East

Sile

Tanis

Avaris

Great Bitter Lake

Buto • Sakha

copper, turquoise from Sinai

Nile River Delta

LOWER EGYPT

Sais

Bubastis

Raqote •

natron

Kom-el-Hisn •

Athribis

ebony, gold, ivory, animal skins incense, gum from East Africa

Ostrich eggs from North Africa

natron

Heliopolis

quartzite, limestone

Wadi Natrun

Abu Rawash

Giza

Zawyet el-Aryan

Abusir

Memphis

copper

Saqqara

Dahshur

el-Lisht

basalt, dolerite, gypsum

Seila

Maidum

Birket Qarun (ancient shoreline)

Faiyum

Hawara

el-Lahun

Herakleopolis

2

E G Y P T

flint

porphyry, granite, jasper, lead

Above The Nile lay at the center of life in Egypt. This tomb painting shows a nobleman and his wife hunting duck from a papyrus boat. River fish were speared or netted.

Zawyet el-Amwat

E a s t e r n   D e s e r t

limestone

Hermopolis

el-Amarna

alabaster

Dara

Asyut

Nile

Akhmim

copper

granite

Koptos

Naqada

Tukh

Karnak

Abydos

limestone

Valley of the Kings

Thebes

Armant

Karnak

U P P E R   E G Y P T

limestone

El-Kab

Hierakonpolis

El-Kula

Edfu

gold, feldspar, emeralds

to the Red Sea

ebony, gold, ivory, animal skins, incense, gum from East Africa

conjectural border of kingdom of Upper Egypt, c.3000

military expansion of Upper Egypt, c.3000

Royal tomb, c.3250–2649

southern border of Old Kingdom

Old and Middle Kingdom pyramids

New Kingdom Royal tombs

New Kingdom temples

Avaris — Royal capital at some point

fertile area

gold — source of commodity

trade route into Egypt

0 ——— 300 km

0 ——— 200 mi

3

W e s t e r n   D e s e r t

alum

El-Kharga Oasis

Kurkur Oasis

amethyst

4

Elephantine

1st Cataract

lead, granite, diorite, steatite, quartzite

Nile

to Nubia

Left The three famous pyramids at Giza. The Great Pyramid of king Cheops (Khufu) is on the right. It stands 479 feet (146 meters) high and was topped with a gilded capstone to catch the sun's rays.

ebony, gold, ivory, slaves from Nubia

UPPER NUBIA

ensured that the king's body continued as a home for his soul. It was solemnly interred in the burial chamber, right at the center of the pyramid. The walls were inscribed with sacred texts and spells, and the chamber was furnished with luxurious possessions for the king to use in the afterlife. After the king's funeral, the entrance passage to the chamber was sealed with stones to protect it from robbers.

Contrary to popular belief, the pyramids were not built by slaves but by skilled craftsmen, helped by peasant farmers during the flood season, when no work could be done in the fields. No one knows exactly how the thousands of heavy stone blocks used to construct the pyramids were lifted into place. Pyramids were very expensive, and none were built after the end of the Middle Kingdom. Later Egyptian kings preferred to show off their wealth and power by building temples, which they endowed with monumental sculptures and carvings.

DEATH & THE AFTERLIFE

The Egyptians called their version of paradise "the field of reeds," a place just like the Nile valley where all the good things of life grew in abundance. Entry to this world was controlled by Osiris, the god of crops and annual rebirth. He was also the judge of souls—only those who had lived good lives could enter the afterlife. The journey to the underworld was a hazardous one. Spells were performed to make sure the deceased would pass safely through its trials. Funeral rites were highly elaborate—by the time of the New Kingdom, the procedure for embalming the body took 70 days. The most important ritual was "opening the mouth," when priests returned the soul to the mummy by touching it with sacred instruments and rubbing its face with milk.

Men of wealth and substance began to build their tombs as soon as they reached maturity. The chambered tomb would be their eternal home in the afterlife, so they furnished it lavishly with food, drink, rich furniture, jewelry, and all the other luxuries they would need. Provision was made for their wives as well. The walls were decorated with scenes of everyday life such as harvesting crops, hunting by the Nile, feasting, and making offerings to the gods. These would magically come alive after death. Models of their cattle and other possessions were placed in the tomb, together with small magical dolls, known as "shabti," who would act as servants and do manual work.

Right Priests open the mouth of a mummy.

INVASION & REVIVAL

Around 1640 BC the Middle Kingdom collapsed and was followed by a period of division known as the Second Intermediate Period (1640–1532 BC). Lower Egypt was conquered by the Hyksos, invaders who probably came from the area of Palestine. At this time Egypt was less developed than its Middle Eastern neighbors. The Hyksos introduced tools and weapons made of bronze, horses, wheeled vehicles (including war chariots), and other innovations. By the time the Hyksos were expelled, at the start of the New Kingdom (1532–1070 BC), Egypt had caught up.

There followed a period of prosperity and expansion when ancient Egypt reached the peak of its power. The New Kingdom rulers were empire builders who extended their authority across the Sinai desert into the Middle East and southward down the Nile far into Nubia, a source of slaves and gold. They exchanged diplomatic letters with their fellow rulers in Mesopotamia, and exercised power over small local states in Palestine. They made Thebes their capital and were buried in underground tombs in an isolated valley on the west side of the

Left The New Kingdom pharaohs had huge statues made of themselves, carved from granite.

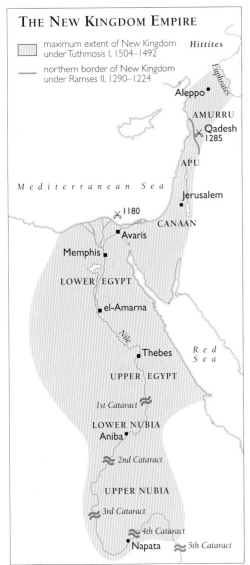

THE NEW KINGDOM EMPIRE

- maximum extent of New Kingdom under Tuthmosis I, 1504–1492
- northern border of New Kingdom under Ramses II, 1290–1224

Hittites

Euphrates

Aleppo •

AMURRU

✕ Qadesh 1285

APU

Mediterranean Sea

Jerusalem •

✕ 1180

CANAAN

■ Avaris

Memphis ■

LOWER EGYPT

■ el-Amarna

Nile

Red Sea

■ Thebes

UPPER EGYPT

1st Cataract ≈

LOWER NUBIA
Aniba •

2nd Cataract ≈

UPPER NUBIA

3rd Cataract ≈

4th Cataract ≈
• Napata   5th Cataract ≈

Nile, known as the Valley of the Kings. They began to call themselves "pharaohs." The title, meaning "Great Palace," symbolized their place at the center of government.

The New Kingdom reached its fullest extent under Tuthmosis I (1504–1492 BC), who took Egyptian power as far as the river Euphrates in Syria. These possessions were later lost, though Ramses II (1290–1224 BC) attempted to restore them. His lack of success did not deter him from building numerous temples and erecting huge statues of himself. The boy-king Tutankhamen (1333–1323 BC) exercised little power during his lifetime but is famous for the rich treasures discovered in his tomb in the Valley of the Kings, excavated in the 1920s.

THE DECLINE OF EGYPT

Though an Egyptian navy succeeded in driving off an attempted invasion by the Sea Peoples in 1180 BC (see page 39), Egyptian power collapsed at the end of the New Kingdom. Some pharaohs even had trouble in paying for their tombs. There was a temporary revival of power under Shoshenq I (945–924 BC) but not enough to stave off Egypt's eventual defeat. It was conquered in turn by Nubians, Assyrians, and Persians before falling to the army of Alexander the Great in 332 BC (see page 46).

(see page 39)
(see page 46)

TIMETABLE

c.6000
Farming begins in the Nile valley

c.3300–3100
The first towns develop. The hieroglyphic script is invented

c.3000
Upper and Lower Egypt are united into a single kingdom

c.2630
The first pyramid is built for king Djoser at Saqqara

2649–2134 OLD KINGDOM

2575–2465
During the 4th Dynasty, royal power increases dramatically

2134–2040
First Intermediate Period
Egypt is divided into two kingdoms

2040–1640 MIDDLE KINGDOM

2040
Mentuhotpe II reunites Egypt

1640–1532
Second Intermediate Period
The Hyksos occupy Lower Egypt

1532–1070 NEW KINGDOM

1504–1492
The Egyptian empire is at its fullest extent under Tuthmosis I

1285
Ramses II claims a victory at Qadesh against the Hittites but loses the war

1070–712
Third Intermediate Period
Egyptian power is in decline

924
Shoshenq I invades Israel and Judah

c.828–712
Egypt is divided into five kingdoms

712–332 LATE PERIOD

712
Egypt is ruled by Nubian kings

671
The Assyrians conquer Egypt

525
The Persians conquer Egypt

332
Egypt falls to Alexander the Great

LANDS OF THE BIBLE

THE ISRAELITES, THE ANCESTORS OF THE JEWISH PEOPLE, PROBABLY
SETTLED IN CANAAN, THE AREA OF THE MIDDLE EAST THAT FORMS THE
LANDS OF THE BIBLE, IN THE 12TH CENTURY BC. THOUGH NOT AS POWER-
FUL AS MESOPOTAMIA AND EGYPT, THE ANCIENT KINGDOM OF ISRAEL HAD
LASTING IMPORTANCE IN WORLD HISTORY. UNLIKE THEIR NEIGHBORS, THE
ISRAELITES HAD ONLY ONE GOD, YAHWEH. THEIR RELIGION WAS TO HAVE
GREAT INFLUENCE ON BOTH
CHRISTIANITY AND ISLAM.

The history and founding
myths of the Jewish people are
recorded in the Bible. This places
their origins in Mesopotamia and describes
their early wanderings through the Fertile
Crescent. According to the Bible narrative,
the Israelites, as they are called at this period, endured a long period of captivity in
Egypt but were led from there by Moses
through the Sinai desert and into the
"promised land" of Canaan. Under their
war leader, Joshua, they conquered most of
the native Canaanite peoples. One famous
story recounts that the walls of Jericho tum-
bled to the ground when Joshua ordered
his men to blow their trumpets.

The Israelites settled in tribal units, ruled
by chieftains called "judges." They were
opposed by the Philistines, a warlike people
who lived near Gaza in the southern coastal

Above Images of calfs
and bulls like this one
from Phoenicia were
widely worshiped in
the Middle East. The
Israelites in the desert
made a golden calf but
were punished for it.

Below The valley of
Jezreel was a major
route from north to east
and the scene of many
battles. In the dry
season it was ideal
terrain for the deploy-
ment of war chariots.

plain, and decided to resist them by com-
ing together under one leader. They chose
Saul (c.1020–1006 BC) as their king. Saul's
successor David (1006–965 BC) defeated
the Philistines and other neighboring states
such as Moab and Edom. These became
vassal, or subject, states of Israel. The last
Canaanite stronghold to be captured was
Jerusalem, which became David's capital.

We cannot be certain how accurate
the Biblical account is, but there is supporting archeological evidence for the
story of the conquest of Canaan and the
foundation of Saul's kingdom. David's military successes may have owed something
to the fact that Egypt and Mesopotamia
had problems of their own at this time and
were unable to stop him.

David was succeeded as king by his son
Solomon (965–928 BC). Solomon's reign
was peaceful and he was able to concen-
trate on lavish building projects. The most
important was a temple in Jerusalem to
house the sacred Ark of the Covenant—the
holy laws given to Moses on Mount Sinai by
Yahweh. But the cost of Solomon's buildings was enormous and this made him
unpopular with his people, many of whom
were forced against their will to work on
their construction. He was blamed for giving land to the Phoenician city of Tyre, to
the north of Israel, in exchange for craftsmen and building supplies. He was also
said to participate in the worship of other
gods as well as Yahweh.

DISUNITY & DIVISION

After Solomon's death the northern tribes
of Israel complained about their treatment
to his successor Rehoboam (928–911 BC).
When he refused to listen, a rebellion broke

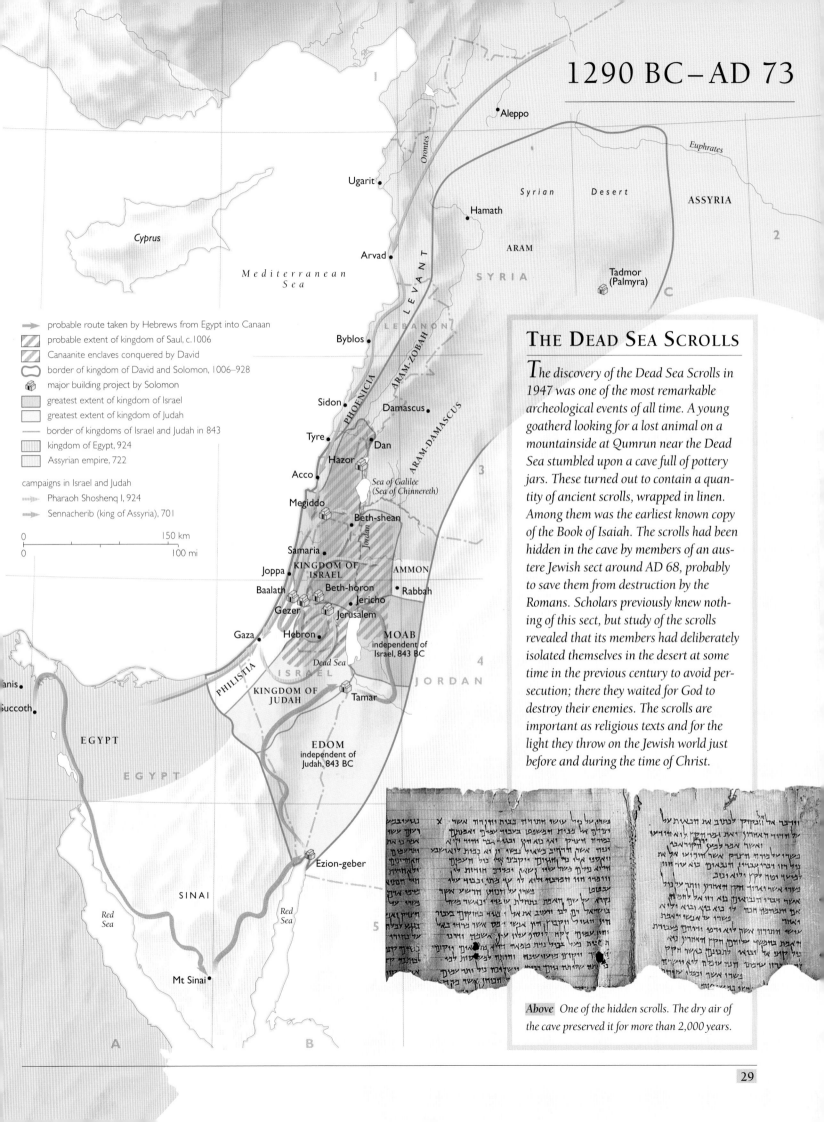

Aleppo

Euphrates

Orontes

Ugarit

Syrian   Desert

ASSYRIA

Hamath

ARAM

SYRIA

Arvad

Tadmor
(Palmyra)

*Mediterranean
Sea*

Cyprus

LEVANT

LEBANON

Byblos

ARAM-ZOBAH

Sidon

Damascus

Tyre

Dan

PHOENICIA

Hazor

ARAM-DAMASCUS

Acco

*Sea of Galilee
(Sea of Chinnereth)*

Megiddo

Beth-shean

Jordan

Samaria

KINGDOM OF
ISRAEL

AMMON

Joppa

Baalath

Beth-horon

Rabbah

Gezer

Jericho

Jerusalem

MOAB
independent of
Israel, 843 BC

Gaza

Hebron

Dead Sea

ISRAEL

KINGDOM OF
JUDAH

JORDAN

PHILISTIA

Tamar

Tanis

Succoth

EGYPT

EGYPT

EDOM
independent of
Judah, 843 BC

Ezion-geber

SINAI

*Red
Sea*

*Red
Sea*

Mt Sinai

→ probable route taken by Hebrews from Egypt into Canaan
▨ probable extent of kingdom of Saul, c.1006
▨ Canaanite enclaves conquered by David
⬡ border of kingdom of David and Solomon, 1006–928
⬛ major building project by Solomon
▨ greatest extent of kingdom of Israel
▢ greatest extent of kingdom of Judah
— border of kingdoms of Israel and Judah in 843
▨ kingdom of Egypt, 924
▨ Assyrian empire, 722

campaigns in Israel and Judah
⇢ Pharaoh Shoshenq I, 924
⇢ Sennacherib (king of Assyria), 701

0		150 km
0		100 mi

THE DEAD SEA SCROLLS

*T*he discovery of the Dead Sea Scrolls in
1947 was one of the most remarkable
archeological events of all time. A young
goatherd looking for a lost animal on a
mountainside at Qumrun near the Dead
Sea stumbled upon a cave full of pottery
jars. These turned out to contain a quan-
tity of ancient scrolls, wrapped in linen.
Among them was the earliest known copy
of the Book of Isaiah. The scrolls had been
hidden in the cave by members of an aus-
tere Jewish sect around AD 68, probably
to save them from destruction by the
Romans. Scholars previously knew noth-
ing of this sect, but study of the scrolls
revealed that its members had deliberately
isolated themselves in the desert at some
time in the previous century to avoid persecution; there they waited for God to
destroy their enemies. The scrolls are
important as religious texts and for the
light they throw on the Jewish world just
before and during the time of Christ.

Above One of the hidden scrolls. The dry air of
the cave preserved it for more than 2,000 years.

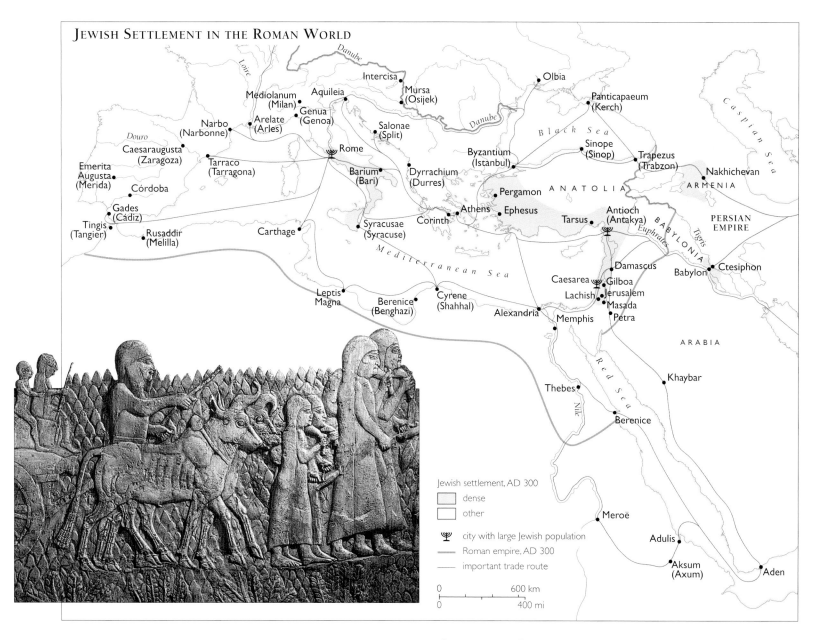

Douro

Loire

Danube

Intercisa

Mediolanum (Milan)
Aquileia
Mursa (Osijek)

Narbo (Narbonne)
Arelate (Arles)
Genua (Genoa)

Salonae (Split)

Olbia

Panticapaeum (Kerch)

Caspian Sea

Caesaraugusta (Zaragoza)
Tarraco (Tarragona)

Rome

Black Sea

Byzantium (Istanbul)

Sinope (Sinop)

Trapezus (Trabzon)

ARMENIA

Nakhichevan

Emerita Augusta (Merida)

Córdoba

Barium (Bari)

Dyrrachium (Durres)

ANATOLIA

PERSIAN EMPIRE

Gades (Cádiz)

Pergamon

Athens
Ephesus

Tarsus

Antioch (Antakya)

BABYLONIA

Euphrates

Tigris

Tingis (Tangier)

Rusaddir (Melilla)

Carthage

Corinth

Syracusae (Syracuse)

Mediterranean Sea

Damascus

Caesarea
Lachish
Gilboa
Jerusalem
Masada
Petra

Babylon

Ctesiphon

Leptis Magna

Berenice (Benghazi)

Cyrene (Shahhal)

Alexandria

Memphis

ARABIA

Khaybar

Thebes

Red Sea

Nile

Berenice

Jewish settlement, AD 300
☐ dense
☐ other

♆ city with large Jewish population
— Roman empire, AD 300
— important trade route

0   600 km
0   400 mi

Meroë

Adulis

Aksum (Axum)

Aden

Above *The first recorded deportation of Jews from their homeland took place at the hands of the Assyrian king Sennacherib who invaded Judah in 701 BC. This carved relief from the Assyrian palace of Nineveh shows Jews being marched out of the city of Lachish.*

out. As a result, the kingdom split into two parts—Israel in the north and Judah in the south, each ruled by its own king.

It was a dangerous time for the Israelites to have fallen out. The pharaoh Shoshenq had brought about a temporary revival in the declining fortunes of Egypt (see page 27). In 924 BC he invaded Judah and Israel and destroyed many cities, compelling the Israelites to pay tribute. However, they continued to quarrel with each other. The vassal states of Moab and Edom seized the opportunity to rebel successfully against their rule. The Bible also tells us that the kingdoms were further weakened by religious disputes. For example, king Ahab of Israel (873–852 BC) is said to have tried to introduce the worship of Baal, a Phoenician god. Religious leaders, known as prophets, such as Elijah and Elisha, warned against the dangers of heresy and internal division.

ASSYRIA & BABYLON

During the 9th and 8th centuries BC the main threat to the Israelite kingdoms came from Assyria, now the strongest power in the Middle East. Israel and Judah were both forced to become vassal states. Rebellions occasionally took place, but were fiercely put down, and large numbers of captives deported to Assyria.

Assyrian power collapsed in 612 BC and was immediately followed by Babylonian rule (see page 23). In 597 BC a rebellion in Judah was ruthlessly put down by the Babylonian king Nebuchadnezzar II. Jerusalem was sacked, the temple of Solomon destroyed, and its treasures plundered. Thousands of Jews (as the Israelites were now known) were deported to Babylon.

During their years of exile, the Jews were comforted and supported by their religion.

Right *The fortress of Masada, built at the tip of a steep outcrop of rock, was the site of a heroic last stand of Jewish rebels against Roman rule. When the Romans stormed the fortress after a three-year siege, the last handful of defenders killed themselves rather than surrender.*

It helped them to maintain their identity as a people while living in a foreign land. It was at this time that most of the books of the Old Testament of the Bible were written down in their present form.

THE JEWISH DIASPORA

King Cyrus of Persia destroyed the Babylonian empire in 539 BC and allowed the Jews to return home (see page 23), though many chose to stay in Babylon. The Jewish kingdoms were ruled first by Persia, then by Alexander the Great and his successors (see page 46). A Jewish rebellion against imposed Greek customs led to the creation of the independent kingdom of Judea in 142 BC, but this was short-lived. In 63 BC it became part of the Roman empire.

By now the Jews were divided into many different sects. The teachings of one Jewish leader, Jesus Christ (c.6 BC–AD 30), gave rise to a new religion, Christianity. Other Jewish sects such as the Zealots stirred up violent rebellions against Roman rule, but these were always severely dealt with. The Zealots were finally defeated with the fall of the fortress of Masada in AD 73. After this uprising the Romans destroyed the temple in Jerusalem and carried its treasures in triumph through Rome.

After each defeat more Jews were forced into exile. By AD 300 few Jews were left in their homeland, but were scattered across the Middle East and all around the Mediterranean Sea. They settled along important trade routes and in busy trading ports.

The spread of Jews around the world is known as the Diaspora. It continued until modern times because Jews were frequently forced to flee persecution in the countries where they had settled, often at the hands of Christians who accused them of murdering Christ. The Jews remained without an independent homeland until the foundation of the state of Israel in 1948.

TIMETABLE

c.1290–1100
The Israelites flee from Egypt and settle in Canaan

c.1020
Saul becomes the first king of Israel

c.1006
Saul is killed fighting against the Philistines at Gilboa

c.1000
David (r.c.1006–965) captures Jerusalem

c.950
Solomon (r.965–928) builds the temple of Jerusalem

c.928
Kingdom separates into Israel and Judah

c.850
The prophets Elijah and Elisha warn against pagan influences

721
The Assyrians conquer Israel

701
The Assyrians conquer Judah

587
The Jews are deported to Babylon by Nebuchadnezzar

587–539
The key books of the Old Testament are written during the Babylonian exile

539
Babylon falls to Cyrus of Persia who allows the Jews to return home

332–1
The Bible Lands become part of the Greek world after Alexander the Great conquers the Middle East

142
The Jewish kingdom of Judea is founded

63
Judea comes under Roman rule

6 BC
Birth of Jesus Christ

AD 70–73
Thousand of Jews are enslaved and exiled after the Romans put down the Zealot uprising at Masada

PREHISTORIC EUROPE

MODERN HUMANS HAVE INHABITED EUROPE FOR 40,000 YEARS. FOR MOST OF THIS TIME THEY LIVED BY HUNTING AND GATHERING. ABOUT 8,000 YEARS AGO, FARMING BEGAN IN SOUTHEASTERN EUROPE AND SPREAD ALMOST EVERYWHERE DURING THE NEXT 3,000 YEARS. THE INTRODUCTION OF METAL-WORKING LED TO THE DEVELOPMENT OF MORE COMPLEX WARRIOR SOCIETIES, AND TO THE EMERGENCE OF THE FIRST EUROPEAN CIVILIZATIONS.

When the first bands of modern humans moved into Europe from the Middle East 40,000 years ago, a large part of the northern continent, covered by vast ice sheets, was uninhabitable. They survived in areas of tundra and grassland by hunting herds of grazing animals such as reindeer. Where they could, they found shelter in caves, or else made themselves hide tents or huts of mammoth bones. About 10,000 years ago the European ice sheets began to retreat and humans gradually spread northward. Europe was now covered in dense forests, which made hunting more difficult. People came to depend more on plant foods, fish, and small mammals.

Farming entered southern Europe about 8,500 years ago. Groups of people living in Greece and the Balkans began to grow cereals and beans, and to raise sheep, goats, and cattle. Some crops, for example emmer wheat and barley, were almost certainly introduced to southern Europe from the Middle East, but the cultivation of others may have developed independently.

During the next 3,500 years farming spread gradually into the rest of Europe, first into southern France and Spain, and then northward to reach the British Isles and Scandinavia by about 4000 BC. In the extreme north of Europe reindeer herding did not replace the hunting and gathering way of life until well into the Christian era.

EARLY FARMERS

Early farming communities were generally small, consisting of between 40 and 60 people. Houses were usually wooden structures, so have left few material remains. In many parts of western Europe, however, the first farmers built tunnel-like tombs of large stones, known as megaliths, which they

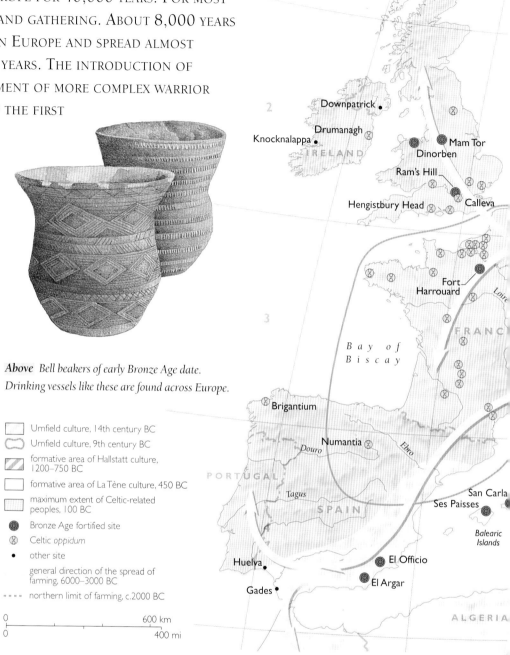

Above *Bell beakers of early Bronze Age date. Drinking vessels like these are found across Europe.*

Urnfield culture, 14th century BC

Urnfield culture, 9th century BC

formative area of Hallstatt culture, 1200–750 BC

formative area of La Tène culture, 450 BC

maximum extent of Celtic-related peoples, 100 BC

Bronze Age fortified site

Celtic *oppidum*

other site

general direction of the spread of farming, 6000–3000 BC

- - - - northern limit of farming, c.2000 BC

0   600 km
0   400 mi

THE DISCOVERY OF THE ICE MAN

When, in 1991, a party of hikers in the Ötztaler Alps came upon a body of a man emerging from a glacier, they supposed it to be that of a mountaineer who had died in a fall. But laboratory testing showed the well-preserved frozen body to be far older. He soon gained the popular name of the Ice Man. Radiocarbon dating confirmed that he had lived around 3350–3300 BC.

Right *The 5,000-year-old frozen body.*

The Ice Man was probably a shepherd or hunter. His ribs had been recently broken, and he may have died of cold and soon after been buried in snow. He appears to have been wearing furs and a cape made of woven reeds, and was carrying many items, including a longbow, 14 arrows, a flint knife, and a small copper ax. Before this exciting discovery, archeologists had not believed metal to be in use in this part of Europe for another several hundred years.

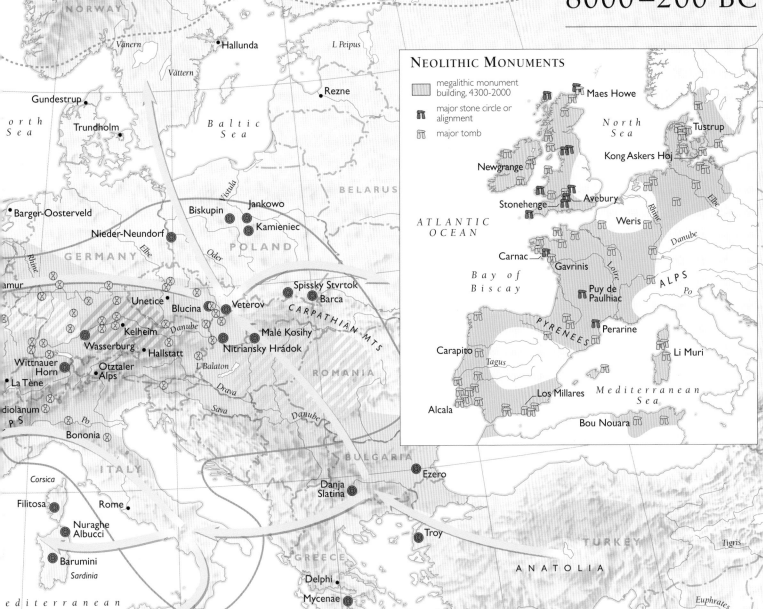

NEOLITHIC MONUMENTS

megalithic monument building, 4300–2000

major stone circle or alignment

major tomb

Maes Howe

Tustrup

North Sea

Kong Askers Hoj

Newgrange

Stonehenge   Avebury

Weris

ATLANTIC OCEAN

Carnac   Gavrinis

Puy de Paulhiac

Perarine

ALPS

Po

Li Muri

Bay of Biscay

PYRENEES

Carapito

Tagus

Los Millares

Alcala

Mediterranean Sea

Bou Nouara

Hallunda   *L Peipus*

Rezne

Vänern

Vättern

NORWAY   *SWEDEN*

FINLAND

RUSSIA

Gundestrup

Trundholm

North Sea

Baltic Sea

BELARUS

Barger-Oosterveld

Biskupin   Jankowo

Kamieniec

Nieder-Neundorf

GERMANY   *Elbe*   *Oder*   *POLAND*

Vistula

Rhine

amur

Unetice   Spissky Stvrtok

Blucina   Veterov   Barca

Kelheim   *Danube*   Malé Kosihy

Wasserburg   Nitriansky Hrádok

Hallstatt   *L Balaton*

Ötztaler Alps

Wittnauer Horn

La Tène

CARPATHIAN MTS

ROMANIA

Drava

Sava   *Danube*

BULGARIA

diolanum

P S

Bononia

Po

ITALY

Ezero

Danja Slatina

Corsica

Filitosa   Rome

Nuraghe Albucci

Barumini

Sardinia

Troy

TURKEY

Tigris

ANATOLIA

editerranean Sea

Sicily

Delphi

Mycenae

Mycenaean civilization 1600–1200

Euphrates

Cyprus

SYRIA

Borg in-Nadur

Knossos

Crete   Minoan civilization 2000–1400

---

covered with earth and turf. As these chambers held the remains of many people buried over long periods of time, archeologists conclude that they were used for communal burials, and that there were few differences in wealth or status. Later people living in some parts of northwestern Europe began to build large stone circles and alignments known as henges (see insert map above). Their purpose is unclear, though it is probable that they had a ritual and astronomical function. Only a powerful chief would have had the resources to organize the building of an enormous structure like Stonehenge (see pages 18–19).

THE BRONZE AGE

About 4800 BC people in Europe began to make small tools and ornaments out of copper and gold. Once again, this development started in the Balkans. Metal-working also appears to have emerged independently in southern Spain about 1,500 years later.

Early metal objects were valued for their appearance, but were of little practical use as they were very soft. The next stage was to mix small amounts of arsenic or tin with copper. This produced a hard alloy called bronze, which could be used to fashion hard-edged cutting tools. Bronze-working is

believed to have spread to southeast Europe from the Middle East around 2300 BC. As a result, metal tools began to replace stone ones in everyday use.

Craftsmen working in bronze and gold were highly skilled at making fine weapons, vessels for eating and drinking, and jewelry for personal adornment. The metal ores needed to manufacture bronze are found in only a few areas, so exchange became more important. Powerful warrior-led chiefdoms were formed. The building of thousands of hillforts throughout Europe suggests that wars occurred frequently between rival chiefdoms in the Late Bronze Age.

The growth in exchange resulted in greater contact between different groups of people in Europe. Cultural ideas spread rapidly from community to community through the mountain passes and along the rivers of central and western Europe. For example, the earliest archeological evidence of the Urnfield Culture—the custom of cremating the bodies of the dead and burying their ashes in pottery urns in huge cemeteries called urnfields—is found in Hungary around 1350 BC. Over the next 400 years it spread throughout almost all of Europe. Earlier burial practices disappear more or less completely from the archeological record.

Trade was responsible for the rise of the first European civilization, the Minoan, which emerged on the island of Crete in the eastern Mediterranean around 2000 BC (see page 36). Its influence extended to neighboring islands in the Aegean and as far as Egypt. A little later, the warlike Mycenaean civilization arose on the Greek mainland (see page 38). Both had vanished by 1200 BC.

IRON AGE EUROPE

The introduction of iron-working into Europe between 1000 and 750 BC brought far-reaching changes. Iron tools and weapons were harder, and cheaper to make, than bronze ones, and iron ore was much more common than copper and tin ores. The early Iron Age witnessed a revival of economic life in Greece and around the Aegean Sea. Partly through the influence of Greek and Phoenician merchants and settlers, civilizations also began to emerge in Italy and southern Spain. One of the most significant was that of the Etruscans, whose city states in northern Italy were well developed (see page 48).

Above This Celtic object is known as a torc. Made of silver, it was worn around the neck, probably to denote rank.

Left An Iron Age hilltop fort in Wales. Such forts were common in Bronze and Iron Age Europe. Some would have served as tribal capitals lived in by the chief and clan leaders, others as refuges for the farmers of the surrounding country in time of war.

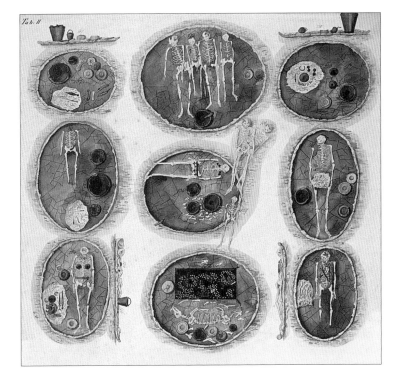

Dominating Central and western Europe were a group of peoples known as Celts to the ancient Greeks and as Gauls to the Romans. They originated in an area of the northern Alps and started expanding out of their heartland sometime after 700 BC. Objects decorated in the Hallstatt art-style (named after an Iron Age cemetery in Austria where it was first identified) have been found across western Europe and into Britain, giving evidence of widespread cultural exchange. Around 450 BC the La Tène art-style developed, which made use of lively animal motifs and intricate geometrical patterns.

From the 5th century BC onward warrior bands of Celts began to invade southern Europe, including Greece and Italy. Much of our information about the Celts comes from the works of Greek and Roman writers, who regarded them as barbarians. They describe them as being given to beer drinking, boasting, and collecting the severed heads of their enemies. Celtic chiefdoms were dominated by warrior elites. Some of their tribal centers, which the Romans referred to as *oppida*, were the size of small towns, with several thousand inhabitants.

Priests, known as druids, were important people in Celtic society. They had many gods, often associated with a particular site such as a sacred spring or tree. Weapons and precious objects were often thrown into bogs and rivers, probably as a form of sacrifice. Human sacrifices were also made.

THE END OF THE CELTS

The Celtic peoples were trapped between two expanding powers. Those living west of the river Rhine and south of the river Danube were overcome by the Romans as they expanded their empire into northern Europe between 225 BC and AD 79. At about the same time, groups of German-speaking people moved into the area east of the Rhine and north of the Danube, extinguishing the Celtic tribes living there. They remain unconquered only in Ireland and the far north of Britain.

Left *A Celtic god from the Gundestrup cauldron, 2nd century BC, found in a bog in Denmark.*

THE MINOANS & MYCENAEANS

THE FIRST EUROPEAN CIVILIZATION, THE MINOAN, AROSE ON THE ISLAND OF CRETE IN THE AEGEAN SEA AROUND 2000 BC. ABOUT 400 YEARS LATER THE MYCENAEAN CIVILIZATION DEVELOPED ON THE NEARBY GREEK MAINLAND. THE MYCENAEANS CONQUERED THE MINOANS BUT WERE THEMSELVES OVERRUN BY INVADERS AROUND 1200 BC. MEMORIES OF BOTH BRONZE AGE CIVILIZATIONS WERE RETAINED IN LATER GREEK LEGENDS. ARCHEOLOGISTS HAVE SINCE DISCOVERED PHYSICAL EVIDENCE OF THEIR EXISTENCE.

Left A wall-painting of boxing boys. It was found in a Minoan house at Akrotiri more than 3,000 years after being buried under volcanic ash and lava. The Minoans appear to have enjoyed all kinds of athletic competition, including bull-leaping.

The Minoan civilization derives its name from Minos, a legendary king of Crete who was said by the later Greeks to have dominated the Aegean Sea with a great navy. Although Crete is a rocky, mountainous island with little fertile land, it owed its early success to farming. On patches of good land in the valleys wheat was grown to feed the island's inhabitants. Vines and olives, native to the region, grew abundantly on the rough hillsides, and the surplus wine and olive oil was traded overseas for valuable products, such as copper, not found in Crete. The Minoans kept flocks of sheep on the high mountain pastures and made the wool into fine cloth, which was exported to Egypt. They also made beautiful painted pottery that was sold abroad.

By 2000 BC Crete had become prosperous. Archeologists have excavated the sites of four great palaces at Knossos, Phaistos, Mallia, and Khania. Each of these palaces was probably the capital of a small kingdom. Vast storehouses in the palaces were filled with grain, jars of wine and oil, and other produce, paid by the farmers as taxes to the king. Food was distributed by palace officials to all those not involved in farming, such as craftworkers, scribes, and traders.

The Minoans were skillful sailors and their ships carried luxury goods all around the Mediterranean. They founded trading colonies on neighboring islands, and even had a trading post in Egypt. We do not know what language the Minoans spoke, but clay tablets found in the palaces are clearly marked with writing. They were probably lists of stores but no one has yet been able to decipher the script, which is known to scholars as Linear A.

FIRE & DESTRUCTION

Around 1700 BC all the palaces on Crete were destroyed by fire. They were later rebuilt, but only one of them—the palace of Knossos—regained its original splendor. A likely explanation is that a war broke out between the kingdoms for control of the island. Knossos was the winner and its king became sole ruler of Crete. The other palaces were reduced in rank, probably becoming local centers of government.

Not much later a still greater disaster occurred. In 1626 BC a massive volcanic eruption blew apart the nearby island of Thera. The Minoan city of Akrotiri on the island was completely buried in lava and ash. It was only found again when archeologists began to dig beneath the layers of ash in the 1960s. They discovered houses complete with well-preserved wall paintings. The scenes on them show that the Minoans were fascinated by the natural world, especially the sea. Similar paintings have been found at Knossos, including one depicting athletes leaping over a bull's horns. This may have been part of a religious ritual. We know that there was a dark side to Minoan civilization, as excavations at Knossos have shown that the Minoans sacrificed children to their gods.

The eruption caused severe damage to the palaces on Crete. This was later repaired

Left The palace at Knossos was discovered at the beginning of the 20th century by the British archeologist, Arthur Evans, who partially restored it. It was the largest of the Minoan palaces, with a maze of multi-storied buildings laid out around a central courtyard. The fine royal apartments were elaborately decorated.

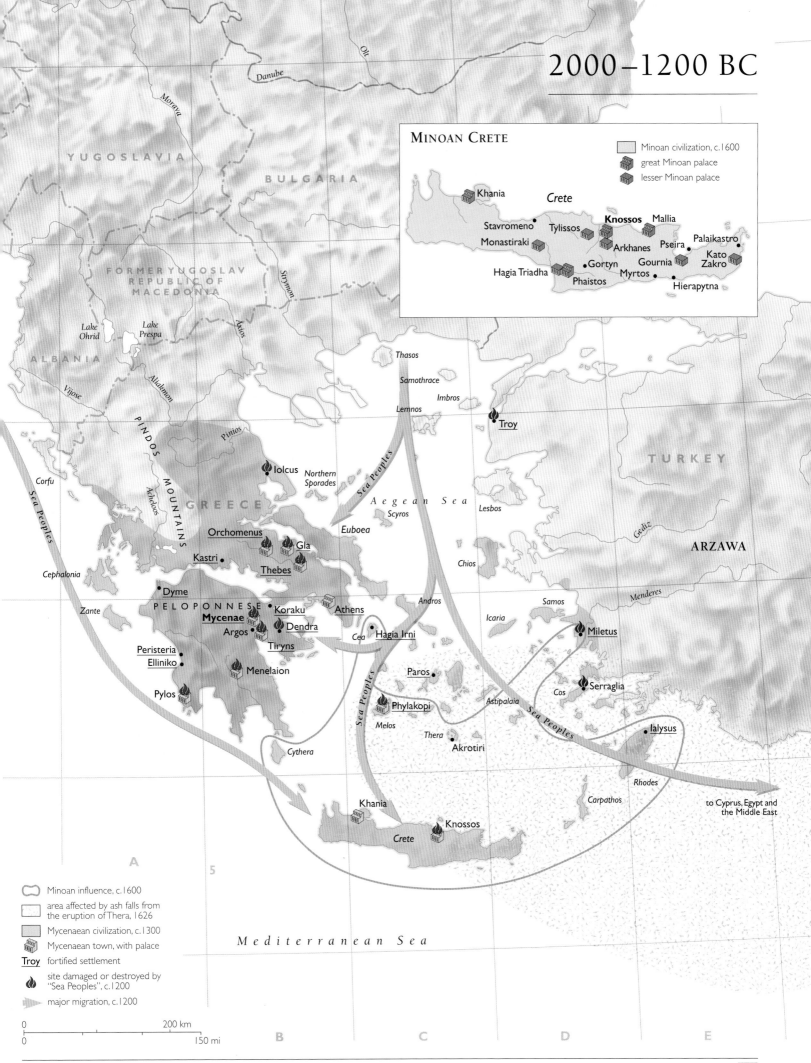

YUGOSLAVIA

BULGARIA

Olt

Danube

Morava

Strymon

Axios

FORMER YUGOSLAV
REPUBLIC OF
MACEDONIA

ALBANIA

Lake Ohrid

Lake Prespa

Vijose

Aliakmon

Pinios

PINDOS MOUNTAINS

GREECE

Corfu

Cephalonia

Zante

Acheloos

Iolcus

Northern Sporades

Orchomenus

Gla

Kastri

Thebes

Dyme

PELOPONNESE

Koraku

Mycenae

Athens

Dendra

Argos

Tiryns

Peristeria

Elliniko

Menelaion

Pylos

Cythera

Thasos

Samothrace

Imbros

Lemnos

Troy

Aegean Sea

Euboea

Scyros

Lesbos

Chios

TURKEY

ARZAWA

Gediz

Menderes

Andros

Samos

Icaria

Cea

Hagia Irni

Miletus

Paros

Astipalaia

Cos

Serraglia

Melos

Phylakopi

Thera

Akrotiri

Carpathos

Rhodes

Ialysus

Sea Peoples

to Cyprus, Egypt and
the Middle East

Khania

Knossos

Crete

Mediterranean Sea

MINOAN CRETE

	Minoan civilization, c.1600
	great Minoan palace
	lesser Minoan palace

Crete

Khania

Stavromeno

Monastiraki

Tylissos

Knossos

Mallia

Arkhanes

Pseira

Palaikastro

Gournia

Kato Zakro

Hagia Triadha

Gortyn

Myrtos

Phaistos

Hierapytna

Legend:

- Minoan influence, c.1600
- area affected by ash falls from the eruption of Thera, 1626
- Mycenaean civilization, c.1300
- Mycenaean town, with palace
- **Troy** fortified settlement
- site damaged or destroyed by "Sea Peoples", c.1200
- major migration, c.1200

0 ———— 200 km
0 ———— 150 mi

A 5 B C D E

Left *Mycenae was built on top of a crag guarding a sweep of hills. The royal palace stood within massive walls, entered through the great Lion Gate.*

Below *This gold death-mask of a king was found in a grave at Mycenae. It was once wrongly believed to have represented king Agamemnon.*

and Minoan civilization continued for a little while longer. It came to an end around 1450 BC when invaders conquered the island and took over the palace at Knossos.

THE MYCENAEANS

The new rulers of Crete copied the art of writing from the Minoans but used their own script (Linear B). Scholars have been able to decipher this script and found it to be an early form of Greek. From this, and from other evidence such as their burial customs, archeologists believe that the invaders were Mycenaeans, a people who migrated into the Greek mainland from the Balkans around 2000 BC. By 1600 BC they had established several fortified cities there. Their name is derived from Mycenae, one of these strongholds in southeast Greece.

Spectacular goods—ornaments of gold, silver, and electrum (a gold and silver alloy), jewelry, and bronze weapons—have been found in several deep graves at Mycenae. They date from between 1650 and 1550 BC and suggest that it was already ruled by kings: such valuable possessions would have accompanied royal burials. Archeologists judge the Mycenaeans to have been a wealthy and warlike people. Their main weapons were spears, swords, and daggers,

and they wore clumsy bronze armor and helmets covered with the teeth of wild boars. They rode to war on horse-drawn chariots, though they fought on foot.

Mycenae was only one—though perhaps the most important—of several small independent kingdoms in Greece. Like the Minoans, their rulers lived in palaces. They were smaller than those on Crete and were strongly defended with walls of huge stone blocks, so large

OVERSEAS TRADE

amber from the Baltic

gold, copper, tin

copper, tin from western Mediterranean

gold, copper, tin

gold

ANATOLIA

Sicily

copper, tin

glass, dye, lapis lazuli, ivory, resins

olive oil

Ulu Burun

Cape Gelidonya

copper

Mediterranean Sea

Crete

Cyprus

ostrich eggs

gold, alabaster, amethyst, ebony, jewelery, linen, ivory

☐ Mycenaean civilization, late 13th century

— Mycenaean trade route

tin source of commodity

🛶 shipwreck

that the Greeks of later times could not believe that ordinary humans had built them—a race of giants must have done so.

The Mycenaean rulers lived in great opulence. The king of Pylos kept 400 bronzesmiths and hundreds of female slaves to weave cloth. Like the Minoans, Mycenaean ships traded all round the eastern Mediterranean and as far west as Italy, Sicily, and Malta. Divers have discovered a ship that was wrecked off the Turkish coast in the 14th century BC. It probably belonged to a Mycenaean king and was found to have jewelry, copper, ivory, ebony, and even ostrich eggs from Africa on board.

THE LEGEND OF TROY

It is more than likely that the Mycenaeans raided as well as traded overseas. We know that they invaded and conquered Crete, and it is also possible that they attacked Troy. This was a powerful city on the coast of Turkey that controlled the entrance of ships into the Black Sea. The legendary story of the Trojan War is recounted by the ancient Greek poet, Homer, who tells of a Greek army, under the leadership of king Agamemnon of Mycenae, which attacked and destroyed Troy after a ten-year siege. Homer's tales of the war—the anger of Menelaus after his wife Helen had been stolen by Paris and taken to Troy, the epic battle between Achilles and Hector outside the walls, the wooden horse built by the Greeks, and the adventures of Odysseus on his journey home—are still read and enjoyed today. Homer lived many hundreds of years after the events he described. However, archeologists have shown that Troy was attacked at least twice in Mycenaean times, and his epic poems may well have been based on folk memories of an actual incident.

THE SEA PEOPLES

During the 14th and 13th centuries BC Mycenaean civilization appears to have been exposed to increasing pressure from marauders from the north. Many strongholds, including Mycenae itself, strengthened their defenses at this time, and a wall was built across the narrow isthmus of Corinth. In about 1200 BC invaders known as the "Sea Peoples" destroyed all the major Mycenaean centers of power. Very little is known about these mysterious people who probably came from the northern Aegean. After attacking Greece, they sailed on to the Middle East and Egypt. Some of them settled in Canaan, where they were known as the Peleset, or Philistines (see page 30).

In Greece, the devastation caused by the Sea Peoples was so widespread that the Mycenaean way of life never recovered. Towns were abandoned and people even forgot how to write. For hundreds of years Greece remained in a "dark age," and very little is known about it.

(see page 30)

THE DIVINE MOTHER

Mother goddess cults appear to have a long history in Greece and the neighboring islands of the Aegean, where enormous quantities of stone and pottery figurines of women have been found, dating back thousands of years. They vary in appearance—some are strikingly simple and geometric in form; others are more shapely with well defined figures. Very often they are nursing babies. We can only guess at their significance, but it is likely that their cult was connected to fertility, crops, and the land—crucially important matters for early farmers.

Several goddesses from later Greek mythology (for example, Ge, Hera, Rhea, Demeter, and Cybele) were associated with the divine mother or crop fertility, and are probably survivals of these earlier cults.

Female figures in Minoan and Mycenaean art often have their arms raised and breasts bared. Sometimes they hold snakes or other objects. They may represent goddesses or priestesses, and evidently had a ritual or sacred function.

Right These figures, representing nursing mothers, are from Cyprus (left) and Mycenae.

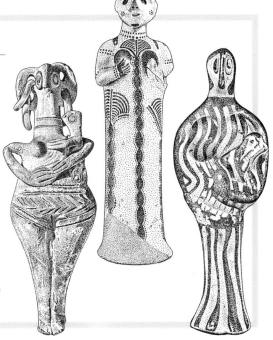

ANCIENT GREECE

THE CIVILIZATION OF ANCIENT GREECE WAS ONE OF THE MOST REMARKABLE IN HISTORY. GREEK ACHIEVEMENTS IN POLITICS, THE ARTS, LITERATURE, PHILOSOPHY, AND SCIENCE STILL HAVE INFLUENCE IN THE MODERN WORLD. YET WARFARE WAS CONSTANT BETWEEN GREECE'S RIVAL CITY STATES.

During the 9th century BC Greece began to recover from the dark age that followed the destruction of Mycenaean civilization. A new wave of invaders, the Dorians, had introduced the use of iron, and urban life revived. Towns developed into independent city-states, which were first ruled by kings. As the opportunities for trade grew, many of these city-states sent groups of citizens overseas to found trading colonies. These colonies helped solve the problem of over-population at home, caused by a shortage of suitable land for farming.

By 500 BC important Greek cities were established along the coast of Asia Minor (Anatolia), around the Black Sea, in Sicily and southern Italy, and as far as southern Spain. The only rivals to the Greeks were the Phoenicians. From their home ports on the coast of Lebanon and Syria they set up colonies in Sicily and Sardinia and along the North African and Spanish coasts.

Most of the Greek city-states had ceased to be monarchies by the 7th century BC and were ruled by hereditary clan-leaders, or aristocrats (the exceptions were Sparta and Argos). The aristocrats gradually came to be resented by other citizens, who wanted a say in how their city-states were governed. Revolutions broke out in many cities to overthrow the aristocrats. These were led by popular leaders, called tyrants, who won support by confiscating land from the aristocrats and giving it to the poor. Tyrants were often harsh rulers themselves, and they too were overthrown as citizens came to demand more power for themselves.

ATHENIAN DEMOCRACY

The city where the citizens won the largest share of power for themselves was Athens. At the end of the 6th century BC, political reforms gave rise to a new form of government, democracy ("rule of the people"). This enabled citizens to vote on all important decisions, such as whether to declare war or how to spend government money. They also elected government officials and generals, and could vote to exile anyone

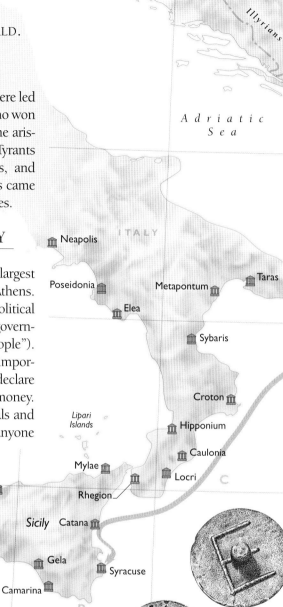

Above Counters were used for voting in the citizen assemblies.

Left The great temple of the Parthenon on the Acropolis in Athens. It was built in the 5th century BC, at the height of the city's power and prosperity.

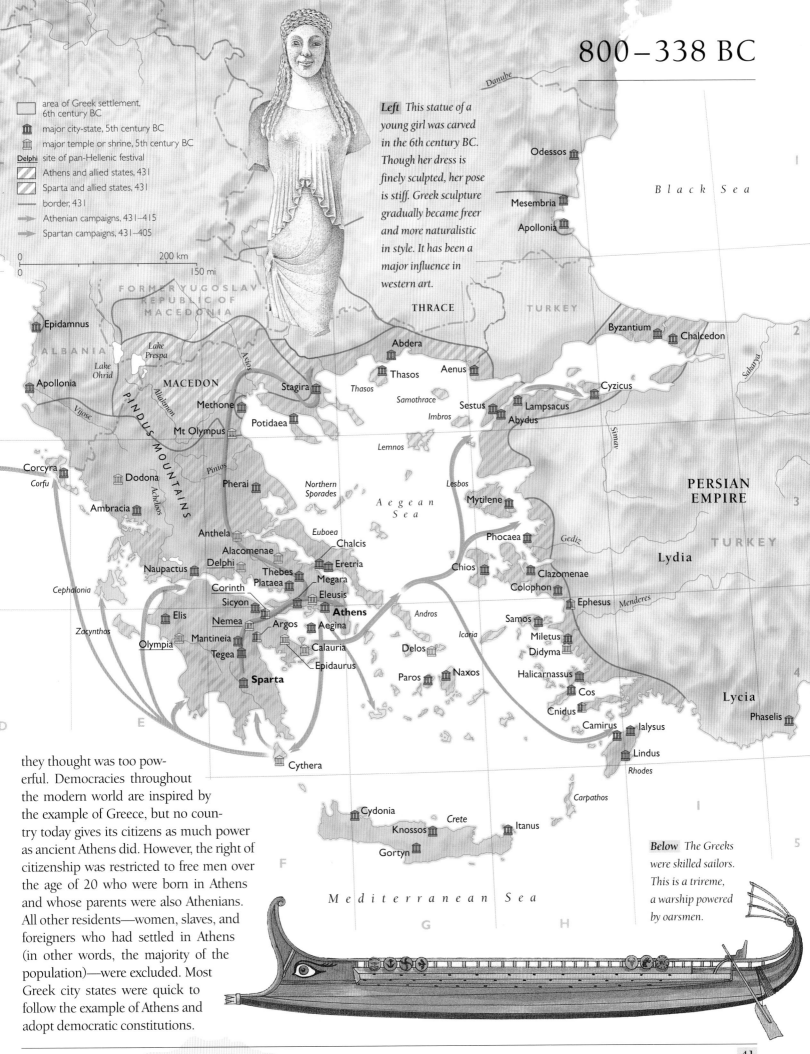

Danube

area of Greek settlement,
6th century BC

major city-state, 5th century BC

major temple or shrine, 5th century BC

Delphi site of pan-Hellenic festival

Athens and allied states, 431

Sparta and allied states, 431

border, 431

Athenian campaigns, 431–415

Spartan campaigns, 431–405

0		200 km
0		150 mi

Left *This statue of a young girl was carved in the 6th century BC. Though her dress is finely sculpted, her pose is stiff. Greek sculpture gradually became freer and more naturalistic in style. It has been a major influence in western art.*

B l a c k   S e a

Odessos

Mesembria

Apollonia

THRACE

TURKEY

FORMER YUGOSLAV
REPUBLIC OF
MACEDONIA

Epidamnus

ALBANIA

Lake
Prespa

Lake
Ohrid

MACEDON

Abdera

Byzantium

Chalcedon

Apollonia

Vijose

PINDUS MOUNTAINS

Axios

Aliakmon

Methone

Mt Olympus

Stagira

Potidaea

Thasos

Thasos

Aenus

Samothrace

Imbros

Sestus

Lampsacus

Abydus

Cyzicus

Simav

Sakarya

PERSIAN
EMPIRE

TURKEY

Corcyra

Corfu

Dodona

Pherai

Pinios

Achelous

Ambracia

Anthela

Naupactus

Cephalonia

Delphi

Alacomenae

Thebes
Plataea

Chalcis

Eretria

Megara

*Northern
Sporades*

Euboea

Eleusis

*Aegean
Sea*

Lesbos

Mytilene

Phocaea

Chios

Clazomenae

Colophon

Ephesus

Gediz

Menderes

Lydia

Zacynthos

Elis

Nemea

Sicyon

Corinth

Argos

Athens

Aegina

Calauria

Andros

Icaria

Delos

Samos

Miletus

Didyma

Olympia

Mantineia

Tegea

Epidaurus

Paros

Naxos

Halicarnassus

Cos

Cnidus

Camirus

Ialysus

Lycia

Sparta

Cythera

Rhodes

Lindus

Carpathos

Phaselis

Cydonia

Knossos

Crete

Itanus

Gortyn

M e d i t e r r a n e a n   S e a

they thought was too powerful. Democracies throughout the modern world are inspired by the example of Greece, but no country today gives its citizens as much power as ancient Athens did. However, the right of citizenship was restricted to free men over the age of 20 who were born in Athens and whose parents were also Athenians. All other residents—women, slaves, and foreigners who had settled in Athens (in other words, the majority of the population)—were excluded. Most Greek city states were quick to follow the example of Athens and adopt democratic constitutions.

Below *The Greeks were skilled sailors. This is a trireme, a warship powered by oarsmen.*

THE GREEKS AT WAR

The city states were fierce rivals for power in Greece and the Aegean, and wars took place frequently between them. The Greeks were tough, highly disciplined soldiers. They carried spears and fought on foot in a tight, defensive battle formation called a phalanx. All fit and healthy citizens who could afford to were expected to buy their own armor and weapons and serve in their city's army when needed.

The finest soldiers in Greece came from Sparta, where all boys were taken away from their families at the age of seven and brought up by the state. Their education consisted mainly of gymnastics and training for war. When he was 20, a man could become a citizen and join a military unit. He could also marry, but he was not allowed to live with his wife and children until he was 30. Even then he had to eat with his fellow soldiers at least once a day.

Their military training stood the Greeks in good stead when the armies of the vast Persian empire tried three times to conquer Greece, by both land and sea. The weather defeated the Persians in 492 BC. Two years later, the Athenian army was victorious at the battle of Marathon. On the third occasion (480–479 BC), Xerxes' huge

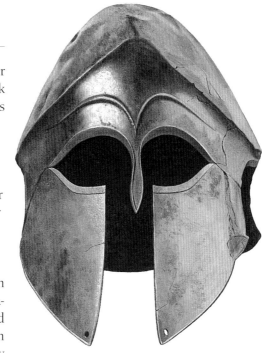

Above Greek soldiers were protected by strong body armor. This bronze helmet would have been crested.

invasion force of 200,000 men and 1,000 ships was vanquished by the combined, much smaller forces of Sparta and Athens.

This show of unity was short-lived. Both Sparta and Athens wanted to dominate Greece. Hostility grew between them as they built up support among the other city states. Sparta emerged victorious from the Peloponnesian War (431–404 BC) that followed, but was not strong enough to keep control for long. As the fruitless wars continued, the city states grew steadily weaker. They were unable to resist the growing strength of Macedon, lying to the north. By 338, its king Philip II, a soldier of genius, had won control of all the Greek city states, including Athens. The classical age of Greek civilization was at an end.

THE GREEK ACHIEVEMENT

Despite their almost constant wars, the achievements of the Greeks between the 6th and 4th centuries BC were unsurpassed in the ancient world. Greek sculptors and painters created artworks of outstanding grace and beauty. The architectural styles of their great columned temples are still imitated. They invented drama and the theater. Greek literature, myths, and legends continue to inspire works of art, literature, and cinema today. The Athenian philosophers Socrates, Plato, and Aristotle are the most important early figures in the history of European thought. The Greeks wrote the first histories, were advanced in mathematics and geometry, and established medicine as a scientific discipline.

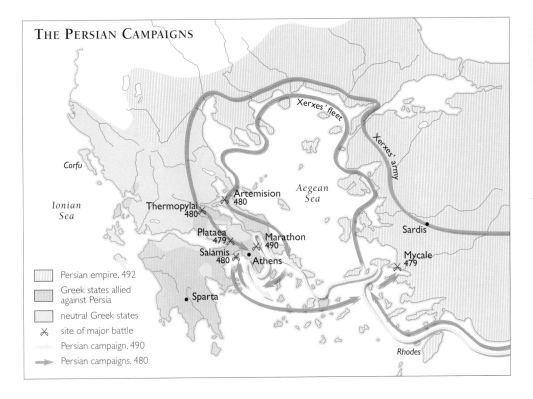

THE PERSIAN CAMPAIGNS

Corfu

Xerxes' fleet

Xerxes' army

Ionian Sea

Aegean Sea

Artemision 480

Thermopylai 480

Plataea 479

Marathon 490

Salamis 480

Athens

Sardis

Mycale 479

Sparta

Rhodes

Persian empire, 492
Greek states allied against Persia
neutral Greek states
✕ site of major battle
...... Persian campaign, 490
➝ Persian campaigns, 480

Little of this would have been achieved without writing. Other ancient writing systems used hundreds of different symbols and took years to learn, but the Greek phonetic alphabet of only 20 chararacters was easily taught. Education had an important function in Greek democracy—politicians could not just do whatever they wanted: they had to persuade their fellow citizens to vote for their policies by skillful argument. Schools were set up to teach these skills, and literacy helped to spread ideas quickly.

High value was placed on physical education, especially athletics, wrestling, and boxing. During great sports festivals like the Olympic games, wars between rival city-states came to a stop to allow competitors and spectators to travel to them safely.

GREEK MYTHS & LEGENDS

*T*he Greeks worshiped many gods and goddesses. Some belonged to a particular place, such as a sacred wood or spring; others had wider significance. The most important were said to live on the top of Mount Olympus in northern Greece. Chief among them were the supreme sky-god Zeus; his wife Hera; Hermes, the messenger; Apollo, the sun god; Aphrodite, the goddess of love; and Athena, the goddess of wisdom. For the Greeks, gods were powerful beings who had humanlike emotions and intervened directly in human affairs. They gave out terrible punishments to those who offended them, but were also ready to help the men and women who pleased them. The highest reward the gods could give a human was immortality. Hercules, for

example, who was endowed with extraordinary strength and performed deeds of bravery, became a god himself.

Every city-state had its own patron god or gods who gave special protection to the city under their care. Sometimes the gods quarreled among themselves over human affairs. During the Trojan War, Apollo sided with the Trojans, Athena with the Greeks. Hundreds of myths and legends were told about the gods. All Greeks were familiar with these tales and would instantly recognize a scene painted on a pottery dish or know what legendary figures were sculpted on the friezes of their great temples. The myths inspired great works of prose and poetry such as Homer's epic poems and the plays of the Athenian dramatists, Aeschylus, Sophocles, and Euripedes.

Left Athena settles an argument about the dead Achilles' armor. A vase painting of the Trojan War.

ALEXANDER THE GREAT & HIS SUCCESSORS

ALEXANDER THE GREAT WAS ONE OF THE FINEST GENERALS IN HISTORY. ONLY EIGHT YEARS AFTER BECOMING KING OF MACEDON, HE HAD CONQUERED THE ENTIRE PERSIAN EMPIRE AND SPREAD THE INFLUENCE OF GREEK CIVILIZATION AS FAR AS INDIA. HIS EMPIRE, HOWEVER, DID NOT SURVIVE HIS DEATH.

Alexander became king of Macedon at the age of 18, following the murder of his father, Philip II, in 336 BC. He was well educated (the Greek philosopher, Aristotle, was his tutor), brave, bold, and violent. As a boy he dreamed of copying the deeds of the Greek heroes Hercules and Achilles, who were the legendary ancestors of the royal house of Macedon. When still a teenager, he had shown great ability fighting in his father's army. With his strong personality, Alexander had the gift of inspiring men to face great hardships and dangers.

DEFEATING THE PERSIANS

Philip II had been on the point of invading the Persian empire when he died. Alexander decided to go ahead with the plan, pausing only to put down a rebellion in Greece first. It was 150 years since the Persians had launched their last unsuccessful expedition against the Greeks, and in this time their empire had grown steadily weaker. However, the present king Darius III was far wealthier than Alexander and could raise enormous armies from his vast empire, which stretched from the Mediterranean Sea to the river Indus.

The size of the empire was not always an advantage. It could take weeks for messengers to travel from one end to the other, and months for soldiers from the provinces to join the royal army. Though huge in number, Persian armies were notoriously difficult to control in battle. By contrast, Alexander's army was well-armed, highly trained, mobile, and skilled in battle tactics. Alexander was a brilliant and inspiring general; Darius timid and unimaginative.

In 334 BC Alexander invaded and conquered Anatolia, liberating the Greek cities along the coast from Persian rule. He had only a small navy and was afraid that Darius might launch an invasion fleet against Greece behind his back. Rather than move deeper into the Persian empire, therefore,

Left Philip II, Alexander's father, developed Macedon's military strength, making it the strongest power in Greece. He was killed at a wedding feast.

he traveled south through Syria and along the Mediterranean coast into Phoenicia, to attack bases where the elite of the Persian fleet was anchored. Along the way he met and defeated two Persian armies, one of them led by Darius himself.

There was little other resistance to Alexander's advance. He was generous to the cities and provinces that came over to him voluntarily, undertaking not to raise taxes or allow his soldiers to plunder them. This was a wise decision as it meant most places were happy to surrender rather than risk a battle or lengthy siege.

The chief Phoenician port of Tyre was one of the few places that refused to surrender. Alexander besieged it for eight months before his soldiers broke into the city. Eight

Persian empire, 336
capital of Persian empire
Macedon, 336
allies and subject states of Macedonia, 336
empire of Alexander, 323
city founded by Alexander (with modern name)
campaign of Alexander, 334–324

0   600 km
0   400 mi

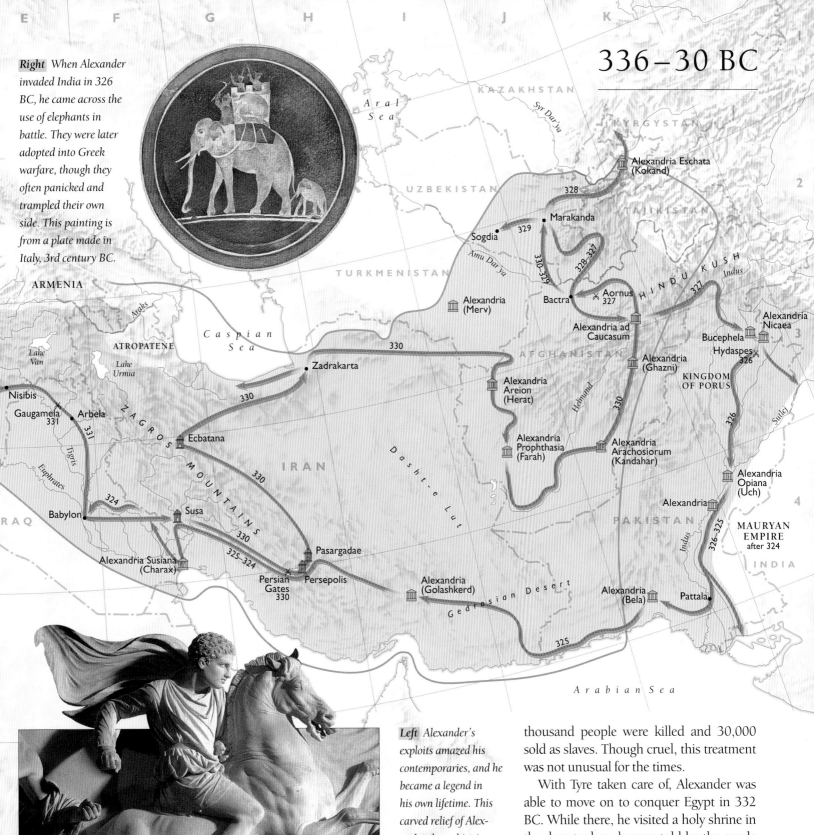

Right When Alexander invaded India in 326 BC, he came across the use of elephants in battle. They were later adopted into Greek warfare, though they often panicked and trampled their own side. This painting is from a plate made in Italy, 3rd century BC.

Left Alexander's exploits amazed his contemporaries, and he became a legend in his own lifetime. This carved relief of Alexander shows him in a heroic pose while out hunting. It is from the frieze of a monument raised to his memory by the king of Sidon (Phoenicia). The frieze depicts Alexander performing many deeds of courage in battle, providing a pattern for others to imitate.

thousand people were killed and 30,000 sold as slaves. Though cruel, this treatment was not unusual for the times.

With Tyre taken care of, Alexander was able to move on to conquer Egypt in 332 BC. While there, he visited a holy shrine in the desert where he was told by the oracle that he was not the son of Philip but had been fathered by Zeus, the most important of the Greek gods. Because of his remarkable achievements, many people—including Alexander himself—began to believe that he really was a god.

In 331 BC Alexander left Egypt to invade the heartland of the Persian empire. At Gaugamela in Assyria he defeated Darius a second time in battle before going on to capture Babylon. Soon afterward Alexander entered Persepolis, the chief residence and capital of the Persian kings, and burned it to the ground. Giving up all hope, Darius fled and was murdered soon after.

THE LAST CAMPAIGNS

For the next three years Alexander's army campaigned ceaselessly in central Asia to complete the conquest of the Persian empire. This was achieved by 327 BC, and Alexander then decided to invade northern India. He won a battle over an Indian king on the river Hydaspes in 326 BC, but by now his army had had enough. Alexander was forced to agree to their demands to return home. They followed the course of the river Indus to the Arabian Sea and then embarked on a grueling journey across the desert to reach Babylon in 324 BC.

Alexander was planning a new campaign in Arabia when he died suddenly in 323 BC. Aged only 33, he was an alcoholic and probably insane. Believing himself a god, he had begun to rule like a tyrant, ignoring all advice. He had given no time or thought to creating a central government to hold his vast possessions together. On his death the empire collapsed into chaos. His heirs, a mad brother and an infant son, were soon murdered and his generals, whom he had appointed provincial governors, fought each other in a series of wars to carve out independent kingdoms for themselves. The most successful and long lasting of these were the kingdoms founded by Ptolemy in Egypt and Seleucus in Syria.

ALEXANDER'S LEGACY

Alexander's conquests spread Greek civilization right across Asia to the Indus valley in the Himalayan foothills. Tens of thousands of Greeks emigrated to the dozens of new cities founded in these newly conquered lands, many of them named after Alexander himself. His soldiers grew rich on the treasure looted from the Persians.

The age of Greek cultural dominance in the Mediterranean and Near East is known as the Hellenistic period (from "Hellene," the word the Greeks used to describe themselves). Greece, however, no longer lay at the heart of the Greek world. Under the Ptolemies, Alexandria in Egypt, the most successful of the cities named for Alexander, came to replace Athens as the center of Greek culture. The rulers of the Hellenistic kingdoms were far richer than the Greek city-states had been. They spent their wealth lavishly on buildings such as

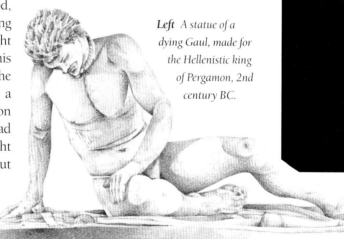

Left A statue of a dying Gaul, made for the Hellenistic king of Pergamon, 2nd century BC.

Above The ruins of Persepolis, in Iran, once the opulent capital of the Persian kings.

the lighthouse of Alexandria, one of the Seven Wonders of the Ancient World. They encouraged new styles of art, particularly sculpture, and extended their patronage to scientists and philosophers like the mathematicians Archimedes and Euclid, and the astronomer Eratosthenes.

The Hellenistic world was overtaken by the rising strength of Rome. Greece and Macedon were conquered in the mid 2nd century. The Seleucid and Ptolemaic kingdoms survived for longer, but they too were ruled by Rome by 30 BC. The Romans had great respect for Greek civilization and borrowed many of its attributes for themselves, including its architecture, science, literature, and mythology.

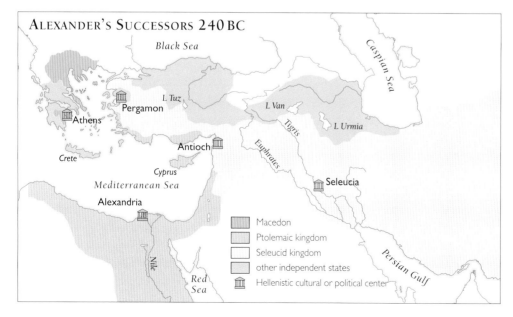

ALEXANDER'S SUCCESSORS 240 BC

Black Sea
Caspian Sea
L Tuz
Pergamon
L Van
Athens
Tigris
L Urmia
Antioch
Crete
Euphrates
Cyprus
Mediterranean Sea
Seleucia
Alexandria

Macedon
Ptolemaic kingdom
Seleucid kingdom
other independent states
Hellenistic cultural or political center

Persian Gulf
Nile
Red Sea

CLEOPATRA: LAST OF THE PTOLEMIES

Cleopatra, the last of the Ptolemaic rulers of Egypt and the seventh queen of that name, is remembered in history as the lover of two Roman generals, Julius Caesar and Mark Antony. But Cleopatra was ruled by more than her heart's dictates. Her actions were driven by political necessity to secure her own survival.

When the 18-year-old Cleopatra became queen in 51 BC Rome had mastery of almost the entire Mediterranean and was waiting for a chance to seize control of Egypt too. She could not hope to remain queen without powerful support, and saw her opportunity in Rome's civil wars (see page 51). Both her Roman lovers hoped to use Cleopatra to gain

Above *Cleopatra wearing Egyptian dress.*

access to Egypt's vast wealth and further their own ambitions. Her plans ended in suicide after Mark Antony was defeated in battle in 31 BC. The dynasty that had ruled Egypt for 300 years died with her, leaving Rome as ruler of Egypt.

TIMETABLE

352–338
Philip II of Macedon conquers Greece

336
After Philip II is murdered, Alexander becomes king of Macedon

334
Alexander invades Anatolia and routs a Persian army at the river Granicus

333
Alexander defeats Darius III at the river Issus (Syria)

332
Egypt is conquered and the city of Alexandria founded

331–330
Alexander returns to Persia. He defeats Darius at Gaugamela before going on to destroy the capital, Persepolis

330–326
Alexander campaigns continuously throughout Central Asia. He wins his last battle at the Hydaspes in India

323
Alexander dies suddenly in Babylon

321–316
Alexander is succeeded by an infant son. His empire breaks up as his generals seize territory for themselves

312
With the capture of Babylon, Seleucus establishes a kingdom in Anatolia, Syria, and Persia

305
Ptolemy proclaims himself king of Egypt and rules in the style of pharaoh

275
The Pharos lighthouse is built at Alexandria (Egypt)

190
The Romans defeat the Seleucid king Antiochus III at Magnesia

148–146
Rome annexes Macedon and Greece

83
The Seleucid kingdom collapses

30
On the death of Cleopatra, Egypt becomes a Roman province

THE RISE OF ROME

LEGEND HAS IT THAT THE CITY OF ROME WAS FOUNDED IN 753 BC. ACCORDING TO THE EARLY HISTORIES, IT WAS RULED BY KINGS UNTIL 509 BC, WHEN THE MONARCHY WAS OVERTHROWN AND THE ROMAN REPUBLIC FOUNDED. BY THE 2ND CENTURY BC ROME HAD TRANSFORMED ITSELF FROM A MINOR CITY-STATE TO THE MAJOR POWER IN THE WESTERN WORLD.

Archeologists believe that the site of the city of Rome was first occupied by Iron Age farmers in the 10th century BC. Urban life seems to have developed there in the mid 8th century BC (about the date of its traditional foundation), and it grew to become one of the largest cities in Italy. The Romans were only one of many different peoples living in Italy at this time. They used warfare and political craft to overcome their neighbors, and by the mid 3rd century BC they controlled almost all of Italy.

EXPANSION OVERSEAS

The strongest power in the western Mediterranean was Carthage, a rich trading city in North Africa originally founded by the Phoenicians. Once it had made itself master of the former Greek cities of southern Italy, Rome began to challenge Carthage for influence in Sicily. This led to a series of

wars, known as the Punic Wars (from *Poeni*, Latin for Phoenicians). Rome emerged the victor from the First Punic War (264–241 BC), with the islands of Sicily, Sardinia, and Corsica added to its possessions. War broke out again over the control of Spain (the Second Punic War, 218–202 BC). The Carthaginian general Hannibal attacked Rome by marching a large army of men and elephants from Spain into France and from there crossing the Alps to Italy. But despite a series of great victories, he was unable to force the Romans to surrender. Meanwhile, a Roman army under the command of Scipio Africanus defeated the Carthaginian armies

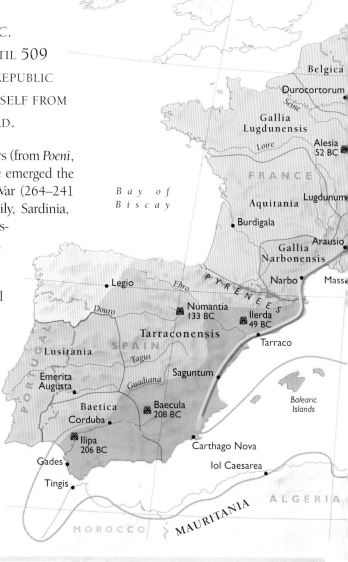

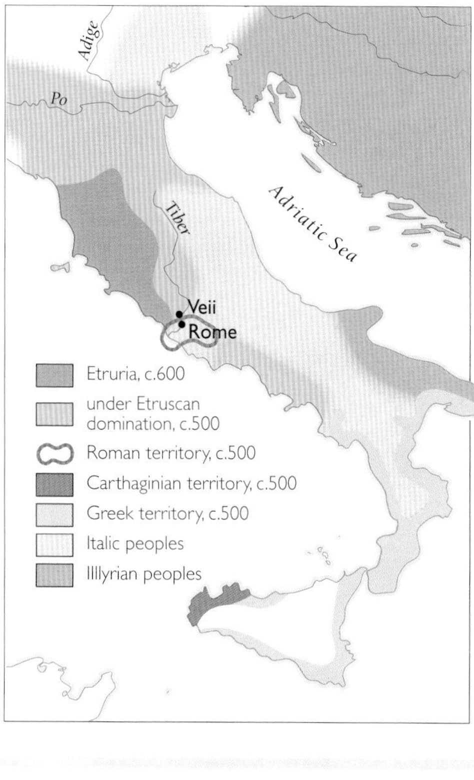

ITALY BEFORE THE ROMANS

Before the rise of Rome, the most powerful people in Italy were the Etruscans, settled in an area approximately equivalent to Tuscany today. By 800 BC they had developed the first urban civilization of western Europe. Active seafarers and traders, they had close cultural contacts with the Greeks and adopted their alphabet. Their inscriptions, however, cannot easily be deciphered, because they spoke a language unrelated to other European languages. Most of what we know about the Etruscans comes from their unique tombs. They built these like underground houses, in clusters or cities, and richly furnished them with grave goods and painted them with scenes of feasting.

Occupying the center of the peninsula were the Italics, a large group of peoples that included the Latins, Sabines, and Samnites.

Above *Tomb statues of an Etruscan couple.*

By 500 BC most still lived in tribes, but city-states had developed among the Latins, one of which was Rome. Once Rome achieved sole cultural and political dominance throughout the peninsula, all knowledge of other Italian languages and cultures disappeared.

Map labels (Spain region)

Belgica
Durocortorum
Gallia Lugdunensis
Alesia 52 BC
FRANCE
Lugdunum
Aquitania
Burdigala
Arausio
Gallia Narbonensis
Narbo
Mass
Bay of Biscay
Legio
Ebro
Numantia 133 BC
Ilerda 49 BC
PYRENEES
Tarraconensis
Tarraco
Douro
Lusitania
SPAIN
Tagus
Emerita Augusta
Saguntum
Guadiana
Baetica
Corduba
Baecula 208 BC
Balearic Islands
Ilipa 206 BC
Carthago Nova
Gades
Iol Caesarea
Tingis
MAURITANIA
ALGERIA
MOROCCO

Map labels (Italy)

Adige
Po
Tiber
Adriatic Sea
Veii
Rome

Etruria, c.600
under Etruscan domination, c.500
Roman territory, c.500
Carthaginian territory, c.500
Greek territory, c.500
Italic peoples
Illyrian peoples

Right According to legend, a she-wolf suckled the twin brothers Romulus and Remus, abandoned at birth. The same legend records that Romulus later founded the city of Rome. This head of a wolf is from a bronze statue, c.500 BC.

Map labels

Germania 12 BC–AD 9
viomagus
Teutoburgerwald ⊗ AD 9
Colonia Agrippina
mania erior
GERMANY
Moguntiacum
Augusta Treverorum
Argentorate
Castra Regina
Augusta Vindelicorum
Raetia
Vindobona
Aquincum
Carnuntum
Noricum
L Balaton
Virunum
Pannonia
Aquileia
Drava
Sava
Tisza
ROMANIA
Viminacium
Singidunum
Novae
Moesia
Danube
Dalmatia
Salonae
BULGARIA
THRACIA
Byzantium
Nicomedia
Sinope
Trapezus
Bithynia & Pontus
Nicopolis ⊗ 68 BC
ANATOLIA
L Tuz
Tigris
Ancyra
Galatia
Asia
Pergamon
Magnesia 190 BC
Ephesus
Tarsus
Carrhae 53 BC
Antiochia
PARTHIA
Syria
SYRIA
Euphrates
Aphrodisias
PISIDIA
Cilicia
LYCIA
Palmyra
Athens
Corinth
GREECE
Creta
Gortyn
Paphus
Cyprus
Judaea
Caesarea
Jerusalem
Macedonia
Pydna 168 BC
Thessalonica
Cynoscephalae 197 BC
Pharsalus 48 BC
Actium 31 BC
Achaea
Brundisium
Tarentum
Pompeii
Rome
Cannae 216 BC
Telamon 225 BC
L Trasimenus 217 BC
Florentia
Italia
Cemenelum
Aleria
Corsica
Sardinia
Carales
Sicilia
Syracusae
Carthage
Malta
Zama 202 BC
Africa
TUNISIA
Leptis Magna
Cyrene
Cyrenaica
LIBYA
EGYPT
Aegyptus
Alexandria
SAUDI ARABIA
Nile
Thebes
Syene
Berenice
Ticinus R ⊗ 218 BC
egusio
Trebia R ⊗ 218 BC
Vistula
Oder
Elbe
Danube
Po
Rhine
Vindelicorum
POLAND
CZECH REPUBLIC
SLOVAKIA

Mediterranean Sea

Legend

▰	Roman empire, c.272 BC
▰	gains by 218 BC
▰	gains by 201 BC
▰	gains by 100 BC
▰	gains by 44 BC
▰	gains by AD 14
▭	temporary gain, with date held
⬭	Carthaginian territory in 264 BC
→	Hannibal's invasion of Italy, 218–216 BC
⊗	Roman victory
⊗	Roman defeat
⊗	Roman civil war
—	Roman provincial boundary, AD 14

0 ____ 600 km
0 ____ 400 mi

still remaining in Spain, and then invaded North Africa. Hannibal sailed home from Italy to defend Carthage but was defeated at the battle of Zama in 202 BC. The city of Carthage itself was conquered and completely destroyed by Rome in 146 BC.

Now undisputed master of the western Mediterranean, Rome was poised to extend its influence eastward. Greece had been invaded in 197 BC, to punish Philip V of Macedon for supporting Carthage in the Punic Wars, and by 146 BC had become a Roman province. In 133 BC Rome acquired its first foothold in Asia with the acquisition of Pergamon in Anatolia (its last king left it to Rome in his will). Bit by bit, Rome took over all the kingdoms founded by Alexander's successors (see page 46). In 30 BC the last of them, Egypt, came under direct Roman control, leaving Rome in supreme command throughout the Mediterranean and Middle East.

ROMAN GOVERNMENT

A major factor in Rome's rise to power was its unique system of government. The city was governed by elected officers called magistrates. They ruled with the help of the Senate, an assembly of former magistrates who decided government policy. The upper classes, who were known as "patricians," dominated the government, but it was possible for talented people from the lower classes ("plebeians") to become magistrates and senators. New government policies were voted on by an assembly of all Roman citizens. The voting system in the assembly was organized in favor of the richer classes, but the plebeians had their own independent assembly and elected their own officers, called tribunes, to represent their interests. In practice, most tribunes were themselves wealthy and used the position as a stepping stone to higher office; for the most part, they had no interest in challenging the status quo. This system of government gave Rome strong leadership, ensured that there was public support for government policy, and helped make the Romans a united people during the centuries of its rise to power.

SOLDIERS & CITIZENS

War was another important factor in securing Rome's success. For the wealthy, military victory brought prestige and the chance to win political power and influence at home. For the poor, it offered plunder and a way to acquire land. Only Roman citizens could fight in the army. At first it was also necessary to be a landowner, but this requirement was abolished in 105 BC. As a result, the Romans were the first people in the ancient world to have a large professional army of well-trained, disciplined soldiers.

Above From the earliest days of the Republic, any Roman citizen had the right to appeal against injustice to the people of Rome. The inscription on this coin of the 2nd century BC reads "PROVOCO" ("I appeal"), and shows a Roman addressing his fellow citizens.

Above The Forum was at the center of life in Rome. Its most sacred temples were here, including the temple of Vesta, which housed the eternal flame that symbolized the heart of the Roman people. So was the Senate house and other important buildings. In the late Republican period, ambitious politicians tried to win popular support by outdoing each other with lavish building schemes for the Forum.

The Romans' unique view of citizenship was a further major factor in their success. In Greece, citizenship depended on birth and was a jealously guarded privilege: this meant that the number of politically active citizens in the Greek city-states remained small. For the Romans, however, all that mattered was residence in Rome; immigrants were welcomed as citizens, and even freed slaves could acquire citizenship. As a result, the number of Roman citizens grew rapidly, and so did the number of potential recruits for the Roman army. Later on, the Romans were prepared to grant citizenship and its privileges to the peoples it conquered in Italy and abroad, if they proved loyal and were prepared to fight for Rome; Roman identity was no longer simply confined to those living in the city of Rome itself. In this way former enemies were brought within the Roman system of government and made loyal citizens.

THE END OF THE REPUBLIC

Its rapid overseas expansion made Rome rich. But it also weakened the republican system of government. Corruption spread as officials tried to keep the wealth of the provinces for themselves. Military conquest brought a huge influx of slaves to Italy, and as a result many poor Roman farmers and laborers lost their lands and jobs. When Tiberius Gracchus, a tribune, tried to introduce reforms, he was murdered in 133 BC.

Ambitious generals became increasingly eager to conquer new provinces and plunder their riches. The wealth they won could be used to buy the support of their soldiers if they tried to win power at home. They were also expected to reward their men with grants of land when they left the army. Soon civil wars broke out between rival generals. In 44 BC the successful general Julius Caesar defeated all his rivals. In power, he abolished the republic and became dictator of Rome. His high-handed actions alarmed a number of conservative republicans, who conspired to murder him.

Caesar's death set the stage for a new civil war. The eventual victor was Caesar's ambitious young nephew, Octavian, who became sole ruler of Rome and its possessions in 31 BC. Under the new form of government he introduced in 27 BC, Octavian, now known as Augustus ("honored one"), became commander-in-chief of the army; he could make laws and reject decisions of the Senate. His official title was *princeps* ("first citizen"), but he had the power of a king. Augustus's rule restored peace and stability to the Roman empire. He was succeeded in AD 14 by his stepson Tiberius. He and all Rome's subsequent rulers used the title *imperator* ("commander"), from which our word emperor comes.

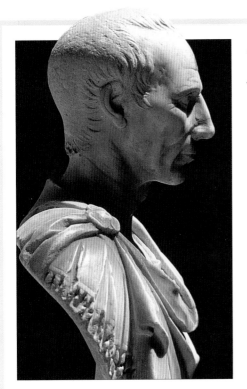

JULIUS CAESAR

Julius Caesar began his political career as tribune, going out of his way to win the support of Rome's lower classes, and then embarked on a conspicuously successful military career. His conquests included Gaul, and he acquired great wealth as well as the devotion of his men. After defeating his political enemies in the civil war of 48–45 BC, Caesar declared himself dictator and destroyed the republican system of government in his quest for power. His reforms improved the life of poorer Romans and provincials, but alienated the Senate. He was murdered by conservative republicans who feared that he was about to make himself king.

Left Caesar was the supreme Roman politician.

EARLY STATES OF SOUTH ASIA

THE INDIAN SUBCONTINENT HAS A COMPLEX HISTORY OF SETTLEMENT. THOUGH IT IS BORDERED ON THE NORTH BY THE HIMALAYAS, THE TALLEST MOUNTAIN RANGE ON EARTH, INVADERS AND SETTLERS HAVE ENTERED THE SUBCONTINENT THROUGH MOUNTAIN PASSES FROM CENTRAL ASIA SINCE EARLIEST TIMES. THE INDUS VALLEY WAS AN EARLY CENTER OF AGRICULTURE AND SAW THE RISE OF ONE OF THE WORLD'S FIRST CIVILIZATIONS. TWO IMPORTANT WORLD RELIGIONS, HINDUISM AND BUDDHISM, ORIGINATED IN NORTHERN INDIA.

The first civilization of South Asia developed on the flood plain of the Indus river, in Pakistan. The environment here was very similar to that of Mesopotamia (see page 20)—the climate was hot and dry, but the soils were fertile, and the river provided plentiful water for irrigation. Agriculture had an early start here, and by 2600 BC the plain was densely scattered with farming villages. In several places small towns and cities had already developed.

CITIES OF THE INDUS

Archeologists first began excavating in the Indus valley in the 1920s. Discoveries at two sites, Mohenjo-Daro and Harappa, gave the first indication that a major urban civilization had existed here more than 4,000 years ago as advanced as those of Mesopotamia and the Nile valley at around the same time. Some cities such as Mohenjo-Daro and Harappa were much larger than other settlements in the region, and may have been the capitals of kingdoms.

It is clear that the Indus civilization was highly organized. The towns and cities were neatly planned on a grid system, with different areas of the city being reserved for specific classes and occupations. They were built on mud-brick platforms to protect them from floods, and possessed a sophisticated water-supply and sewerage system.

We know very little about the people who built these cities. Though stone seals carved with pictographs (see page 16) show that the Indus people could write, the script

Left A small carved head from Mohenjo-Daro. He is thought to represent a priest or king. The bared right shoulder, headband, armring, and trefoil-patterned robe are all traditional signs of holiness in India.

UTTARAPATH

Below Mohenjo-Daro stood on a hill above the floodplain of the river Indus. Built entirely of baked mud bricks, it had a population of 30,000–40,000, making it one of the largest Bronze Age cities in the world.

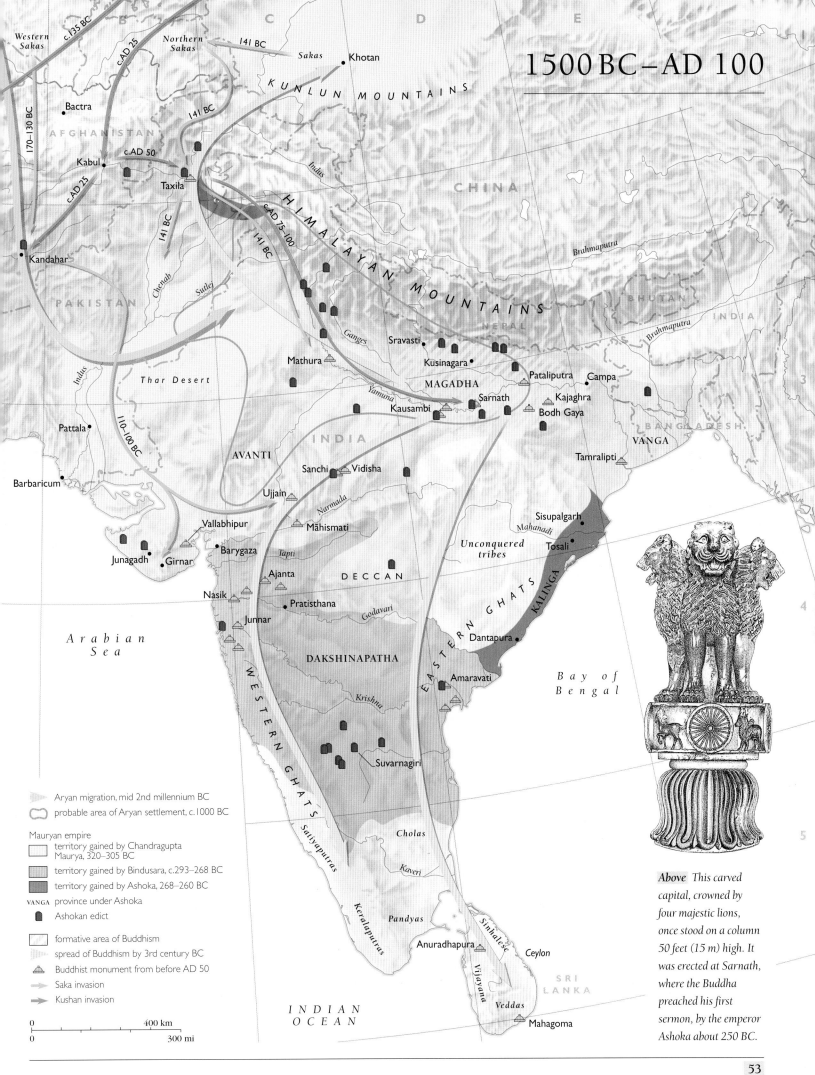

Western
Sakas

c.135 BC

Northern
Sakas

141 BC

Sakas
● Khotan

KUNLUN MOUNTAINS

● Bactra

c.AD 25

AFGHANISTAN

141 BC

HIMALAYAN

CHINA

Kabul c.AD 50

Taxila

Indus

MOUNTAINS

Brahmaputra

BHUTAN

Kandahar

141 BC

Chenab

Sutlej

c.AD 75–100

141 BC

Ganges

Sravasti

NEPAL

INDIA

Brahmaputra

141 BC

Mathura

Kusinagara

Patliputra

● Campa

PAKISTAN

Thar Desert

Yamuna

MAGADHA

Sarnath

Kajaghra

BANGLADESH

Pattala

Indus

AVANTI

Kausambi

Bodh Gaya

VANGA

110–100 BC

INDIA

Barbaricum

Sanchi Vidisha

Tamralipti

Ujjain

Narmada

Sisupalgarh

Mahanadi

Vallabhipur

Māhismati

Unconquered
tribes

Tosali

Junagadh Girnar

Barygaza

Tapti

DECCAN

KALINGA

Ajanta

Godavari

EASTERN GHATS

Dantapura

Bay of
Bengal

Nasik

Pratisthana

Arabian
Sea

Junnar

DAKSHINAPATHA

Krishna

Amaravati

WESTERN GHATS

Suvarnagiri

Satyaputras

Cholas

Aryan migration, mid 2nd millennium BC

probable area of Aryan settlement, c.1000 BC

Mauryan empire

Kaveri

Pandyas

Keralaputras

territory gained by Chandragupta
Maurya, 320–305 BC

territory gained by Bindusara, c.293–268 BC

territory gained by Ashoka, 268–260 BC

VANGA province under Ashoka

Ashokan edict

formative area of Buddhism

spread of Buddhism by 3rd century BC

Buddhist monument from before AD 50

Saka invasion

Kushan invasion

Anuradhapura

Ceylon

Sinhalese

SRI
LANKA

Vijayana

INDIAN
OCEAN

Veddas

Mahagoma

0   400 km

0   300 mi

Above This carved
capital, crowned by
four majestic lions,
once stood on a column
50 feet (15 m) high. It
was erected at Sarnath,
where the Buddha
preached his first
sermon, by the emperor
Ashoka about 250 BC.

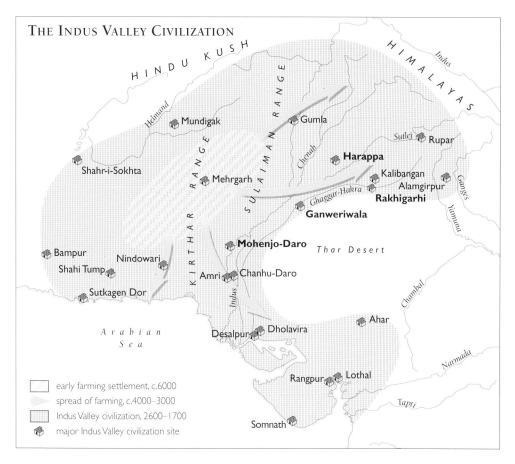

THE INDUS VALLEY CIVILIZATION

early farming settlement, c.6000

spread of farming, c.4000–3000

Indus Valley civilization, 2600–1700

major Indus Valley civilization site

god Indra. They were passed on by word of mouth and did not come to be written down until the 6th century BC.

Central to Hinduism is its caste system, or hereditary system of social ranking. This has developed from the four *varnas* or classes of Aryan society. The two highest classes were the Brahmins, the priestly caste, and the Kshatriyas, the warriors. Next came the Vaishyas, peasant farmers and merchants, with the Shudras, craftsmen, laborers, or slaves, at the bottom. Kings were always members of the warrior class, but they also had important religious duties, such as performing rituals to maintain the fertility of the fields and secure good harvests.

NEW BELIEFS

By 500 BC Hinduism had spread widely through the Indian subcontinent. It taught that each individual has to go through an endless cycle of rebirth. The Brahmins had come to hold great power, and it was partly dissatisfaction with their role that led to the development of a number of new sects, such as Jainism (still practiced by many people in India today) and Buddhism. The founder of Buddhism was Siddhartha Gautama (c.563–483 BC). His teachings gained hold in and around the Gangetic plain, where he lived and died, but did not achieve wider popularity until the reign of the emperor Ashoka (r.268–233 BC).

Below An early Buddhist stupa, or shrine.

has not yet been deciphered and we do not even know what language they spoke. They had extensive trading links reaching far into the subcontinent and along the coast of the Persian Gulf to Mesopotamia.

The Indus civilization appears to have gone into decline about 1800 BC, and by 1700 BC the cities had been abandoned. The reasons for this are unclear, but as life continued unchanged in the countryside, it is unlikely that invaders were responsible. It is possible that repeated flooding or some other environmental catastrophe played a part in their desertion.

VEDIC INDIA

Around 1500 BC the Aryans migrated into northern India from central Asia. They were cattle-owning seminomads, but by about 1000 BC they appear to have settled down as rice farmers on the vast, fertile Ganges plain that extends for 1,900 miles (3,000 km) west to east across the north of the subcontinent. There they developed a village-based society, loosely held together in small tribal kingdoms. By this time they had begun to use iron tools and weapons, which they had probably learned to make independently of outside influence.

The Aryans had enormous influence on Indian history. Many of the numerous languages spoken in India today have evolved from their Sanskrit language. Hinduism, the most widespread religion of modern India, is descended from the Aryan form of religion. The earliest Hindu scriptures are the Vedas, collections of hymns that tell the mythical history of the migrations and wars of the Aryans under the leadership of their

THE BUDDHA

All we know about Siddhartha Gautama, the Buddha (or "Enlightened One"), comes from traditions written down long after his death. They relate that he was born a prince of a small kingdom in northern India. One day, age 29, he took a chariot ride outside his father's palace and saw real human suffering for the first time. Overwhelmed by sorrow, he abandoned his life of luxury. For six years he led a life of extreme austerity, fasting and meditating, until he received enlightenment while seated beneath a tree. The essence of Gautama's teaching was that by following the Eightfold Path of righteous thought and action it was possible to attain Nirvana, a state free of suffering, and end the Hindu cycle of rebirth.

Left A Buddha from Gandhara, in the northwest. It is influenced by Greek art, following Alexander the Great's conquest of the Indus valley.

THE EMPEROR ASHOKA

Ashoka ruled over the Mauryan empire, founded by his grandfather Chandragupta Maurya (r.321–293 BC). Chandragupta was an able administrator and a fine soldier. He made a name for himself as a commander in the northwest of India at the time of Alexander the Great's invasion of the Indus valley (see page 46) and later seized power in Magadha, the most important kingdom in the Gangetic plain. He established strong central government and built roads, irrigation systems, and other public works. Chandragupta brought almost all of northern India under his control. His son Bindusara (r.293–268 BC) extended the influence of the Mauryan empire far into the Deccan, the central plateau of India.

Ashoka began his reign by conquering Kalinga in eastern India. This was highly valued as the source of the best war elephants. However, Ashoka was so horrified by the suffering caused by war that he converted to Buddhism and from then onward attempted to live by its teachings of nonviolence and compassion for all living things. He informed the rulers of neighboring states that they would not be attacked, and gave up hunting and eating meat.

On Ashoka's orders, Buddhist teachings were inscribed on cliffs and stone pillars throughout India. He sent missionaries to Ceylon, Indonesia, and Central Asia, areas where Buddhism would later become very strong, and even as far as Syria, Egypt, and Anatolia. In this way, Buddhism took the first steps to becoming a world religion. But Ashoka also practiced religious toleration. Although many people in India followed his example and converted to Buddhism, the majority were allowed to practice their traditional Hindu beliefs unhindered.

The Mauryan empire declined after Ashoka's death and by 185 BC had split up into several independent states. They were not strong enough to resist new invaders from central Asia, the Sakas (a branch of the Scythians). After them came the Kushans, who controlled a network of states in the north and enjoyed extensive trading links with China, Persia, and Rome. These newcomers adopted the languages and religions of the people they ruled over and were fully assimilated into Indian culture. Meanwhile, thriving ports and independent kingdoms were beginning to emerge in south India as the opportunities for sea trade increased.

FIRST EMPERORS OF CHINA

FARMING BEGAN IN THE YELLOW RIVER VALLEY ABOUT 8,000 YEARS AGO. ABOUT 3000 BC RICE FARMING SPREAD THERE FROM THE YANGTZE RIVER FLOODPLAIN, AND IT WAS HERE THAT THE FIRST CIVILIZATION IN CHINA, THE SHANG, DEVELOPED ABOUT 1766 BC. AS DYNASTIES CAME AND WENT, THE BORDERS OF THE EARLY CHINESE STATE EXPANDED SOUTH AND WEST.

About 3000 BC, as agriculture became more developed and the population began to rise, the first towns and fortifications arose in the Yellow river valley of northern China. According to later legends, Chinese civilization was founded by the emperor Huang Di in 2698 BC. However, there is no archeological or historical evidence for any ruling dynasty before the Shang (c.1766–1122 BC).

During this time, cities developed and a pictographic script, the ancestor of the modern Chinese script, came into use. The Shang kings believed that they could talk to their ancestors by writing questions on special bones called oracle bones. The bones were struck with a hot metal rod, and the resulting pattern of cracks was believed to show the ancestors' answer. The kings took care not to take important decisions without ensuring they had the approval of their ancestors.

The influence of the Shang dynasty was quite widely spread across northern China. Shang rulers were extremely powerful. When a king died, hundreds of his soldiers and servants were sacrificed and buried with him. This meant that he could be sure of being guarded and looked after in the afterlife.

THE ZHOU DYNASTY

The Shang dynasty was overthrown by Wu, king of Zhou, in 1122 BC, who founded the longest lasting dynasty of Chinese history. Observing and interpreting astronomical events for the people was part of

Left *Early Chinese bronze working was the most advanced in the world. Skilled craftsmen could cast incredibly complicated shapes using molds made up of several separate pieces. Vessels like this one of Zhou manufacture were used to make food and drink offerings to the gods.*

the obligations of early Chinese rulers. The Zhou kings claimed that celestial approval for their dynasty's authority was demonstrated through the "Mandate of Heaven." The stars could also predict the downfall of dynasties. All future rulers of China would claim to rule by the Mandate.

Later generations looked back to the time of the Zhou kings as a golden age. However, in 770 BC the kingdom was invaded by nomads from the west. The capital moved from Hao to Luoyang, and the kingdom disintegrated into semi-independent states. This troubled time is known as the Spring and Autumns Period (770–480 BC). It was followed by the Warring States Period (480–221 BC), when the authority of the Zhou kings declined even further.

Despite the almost constant background of warfare, important changes were taking place. Iron came into use around 600 BC, though iron weapons did not replace bronze until the 2nd century BC. Literature and philosophy flourished. The most important cultural development was the creation of Confucianism, the system of ethical beliefs that remains fundamental to Chinese thought and behavior. Its founder, Confucius (551–479 BC), was born at Qufu in Lu province to a poor but aristocratic family. He became a government official before seeking the life of a wandering

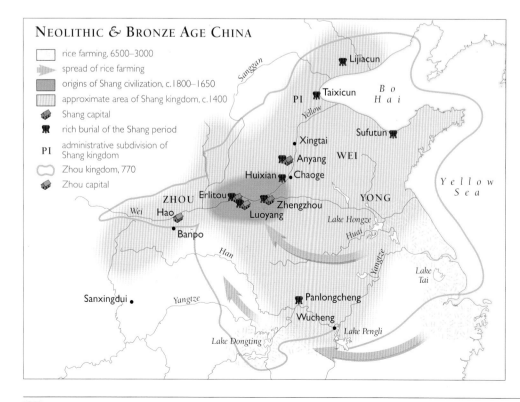

NEOLITHIC & BRONZE AGE CHINA

- rice farming, 6500–3000
- spread of rice farming
- origins of Shang civilization, c.1800–1650
- approximate area of Shang kingdom, c.1400
- Shang capital
- rich burial of the Shang period
- **PI** administrative subdivision of Shang kingdom
- Zhou kingdom, 770
- Zhou capital

MONGOLIA

Inner Mongolian Plateau

Xiongnu (nomads)

99 BC

119 BC

119 BC

175–170 BC

Gobi Desert

127 BC

315 BC

201 BC

119 BC

Yan wall, c.290 BC

Zhao wall, c.300 BC

Xiangping

YAN

NORTH KOREA

Luolang

Yue Qi (nomads)

Shanggu

Ji

Youbeiping

Koreans

Changye

Wuyuan

Ordos Desert

Diangxiang

ZHONG-SHAN

Bo Hai

SOUTH KOREA

Liangzhou

Lake Qinghai

Yellow

ZHAO

Jinyang

Yellow

QI

Linzi

Zichuan

Yellow Sea

Handan

Wei wall c.353 BC

WEI

Pingyang

Puyang

Qi wall, c.450 BC

Ji

LU

Qufu

Jincheng

Yellow

QIN MTS

Qin

Ping

Yong

Xianyang

QIN

Luoyang

ZHOU

SONG

Shangqiu

Tibetans

Chang'an

Pingyang

HAN

Xinzheng

Chu wall

Daliang

Chen

Lake Hongze

Guangling

Jinsha (Yangtze)

Yalong

Dadu

Han

Huai

Juyang

Shouchun

Nanjing

Wu

Lake Tai

SHU

DABA MTS

Yanying (Ruo)

CHINA

Yangtze

CHU

Guiji

Shu

Danyang

Ying

East China Sea

Ba

Lake Dongting

Lake Pengli

Pengli

Independent mountain tribes

Lingling

Guiyang

Viets

Lancang (Mekong)

TAIWAN

Thai-speaking tribes

Yizhou

Xi

Nanhai

Viets

Red

VIETNAM

Black

LAOS

Jiaozhi

Zhuyai

South China Sea

Juizhen

Hainan

Mekong

0 ———— 600 km
0 ———— 400 mi

sage and teacher. Confucius's moral teachings stressed respect for authority, family, and tradition. He instructed rulers to act virtuously so as to set a good example for their subjects to follow.

THE FIRST EMPEROR

After the Warring States Period, the province of Qin, in the west, emerged as the strongest power in China. Its mountainous borders made it hard to attack, and from about 350 BC onward it steadily expanded its territory by conquering the tribal peoples on its western borders. Between 230 and 221 BC the Qin king Zheng, in a series of lightning campaigns, rapidly conquered the other states of China. To mark his success he adopted the title Shi Huangdi, or "First Emperor".

As a defense against nomad invasions, Shi Huangdi linked the border ramparts built in the Warring States Period into a continuous earth barrier that stretched for more than 1,000 miles (1600 km). This was the beginning of the Great Wall of

THE TERRACOTTA ARMY

In 1974, peasants digging a well near the ancient Qin capital of Xianyang broke into a pit containing thousands of lifesize clay soldiers. They had been placed there to guard the body of Shi Huangdi, who is buried in a massive mound about 1 mile (1.6 km) away. Records state that more than 700,000 men were conscripted from all over the empire to build it.

Archeologists uncovered more than 7,000 soldiers belonging to the Terracotta Army, together with their horses and war chariots. Enormous care had been taken in sculpting the figures: the head of each soldier is different, with a wide range of facial expressions, beards, and hairstyles being seen. They include archers, infantrymen, and cavalry, and provide invaluable information about ancient Chinese armor and weaponry.

Right *Terracotta soldiers stand ready for battle.*

Top *A checkerboard of fields in the Yellow river valley. From the Shang civilization to the Han dynasty, this fertile region formed the heartland of the early Chinese state.*

Above *Horses, first domesticated in southern Russia, were highly prized by the Chinese, who would capture fine specimens on their campaigns in the west. This bronze horse and rider from Gansu is of Han origin.*

China, though the stone wall that can be seen today is of much later date.

Shi Huangdi adopted forceful measures to unite his empire. Local customs were banned; everyone had to obey the same laws and use the same coins, weights, measurements, and style of writing. Even the width of axles on wagons had to be the same. The emperor appointed all officials. Opposition to his policies was ruthlessly punished, usually by death.

For a man who did not care how many people he killed, Shi Huangdi was terrified of dying himself. He ordered doctors to try to discover a medicine to make him immortal. They failed, of course, and Shi Huangdi died in 210 BC. The cost of his policies had been enormous. Peasant farmers had been taxed heavily to pay for them, and forced to join the army or work on building projects. In 206 BC a rebellion broke out and the entire Qin royal family was massacred.

THE HAN DYNASTY

Although the downfall of the Qin dynasty sparked off a ferocious civil war, the empire did not break up. The eventual winner was Gaozu, the first emperor of the Han dynasty (202 BC–AD 220). Gaozu recognized that the Qin dynasty had been overthrown because it had been too brutal. He therefore reduced taxes, gave land to the peasants, and passed other reforms to increase prosperity. The law was made less harsh and the death penalty used much less.

China continued to expand under the early Han emperors, who conquered large territories in the south and much of the Korean peninsula. In the west, seizure of the strategic Gansu corridor opened the way to central Asia, where a protectorate was set up. Xiongnu nomads invaded China many times from Mongolia but were eventually defeated in 36 BC. The Han's constant military campaigns drained the economy, and in AD 9 the dynasty was overthrown by a rebel called Wang Mang.

Though the Han won back their throne just 14 years later, they were unable to revive their former greatness. Peasant rebellions became common. The emperors were figureheads only, isolated from their subjects by the ceremonies of court ritual. Actual power passed into the hands of their generals and officials. In 220, the last Han emperor was deposed and the empire broke up into three separate kingdoms.

GLOSSARY

Anatolia The large peninsula of Turkey, also known as Asia Minor, that lies between the Black Sea and the Mediterranean. It was an early center of farming and iron-working.

anthropologist A person who studies the origins, physical characteristics, social organization, and customs of humans.

archeologist A person who finds out how people used to live by uncovering and examining the material remains (dwelling sites, burials, ARTIFACTS, monuments, etc.) of past societies.

aristocracy A hereditary, privileged class of society; a noble elite.

artifact Any object made by humans.

Aryans Nomadic pastoralists from Central Asia who migrated into the Indian subcontinent around 1500 BC.

Assyrians A powerful people of the Middle East named for the city of Ashur in northern MESOPOTAMIA (northern Iraq). The greatest period of Assyrian power lasted from about 1000–600 BC.

Babylonians The people of the city of Babylon in southern MESOPOTAMIA. The first Babylonian empire, which arose around 1800 BC, was destroyed by the HITTITES in 1600 BC. After Assyria declined in 600 BC, Babylonia briefly enjoyed power once again.

Bronze Age The period of Asian and European prehistory, lasting from about 4000 BC–1200 BC, when most tools and weapons were made of bronze. Bronze is an alloy of copper with arsenic and tin. It is harder than copper alone and provides a sharper cutting edge.

Buddhism A religion founded by the Indian mystic Siddhartha Gautama ("the Buddha") in the 5th century BC, which spread from India to Southeast Asia, Tibet, China, and Japan.

Carthagians The inhabitants of Carthage, a major port and trading city in North Africa founded by the PHOENICIANS in 814 BC.

chiefdom A HIERARCHICAL SOCIETY ruled by a leader or CLAN-based elite.

citizen In ancient Greece, a land-owning member of a CITY-STATE. Citizenship was inherited; outsiders, women, and slaves were excluded. Roman citizenship was more inclusive, and could be granted to conquered peoples and ex-slaves.

city-state An independent city that controlled a surrounding territory, large or small.

civilization An advanced form of human society, with complex social structures and cultural achievements such as writing, mathematics, technology, and monumental architecture.

clan A group of people related by common ancestry or marriage.

colony A group of people who found a new community in a distant territory but retain ties with their parent state.

Confucianism A social and moral philosophy created by the Chinese scholar Confucius around 500 BC. It remained at the heart of Chinese society and CULTURE to modern times.

culture The shared ideas, beliefs, values, and knowledge of a particular society; the material goods (ARTIFACTS) that are produced by that society.

cuneiform The "wedge-shaped" writing used in MESOPOTAMIA from the 3rd to the late 1st millennium BC.

democracy In ancient Greece, the direct government of a CITY-STATE by the CITIZEN body.

domestication The adaptation of wild plants or animals through selective breeding to make them useful for humans.

dynasty A ruling family or other group that holds power for several generations.

Etruscans A people of north-central Italy, of unknown origin, who developed a distinctive culture in the 8th century BC. They were conquered by the Romans in the 4th century BC.

Fertile Crescent A region of good soil stretching in an arc from modern Israel through Lebanon, Syria, southern ANATOLIA, and Iraq to the Persian Gulf. It was here that settled farming began 10,000 years ago.

fossil The remains of any animal or plant that have been preserved in sedimentary mud or rock.

Han The ruling dynasty of China from 206 BC–AD 220. It is also the name of the Chinese people.

Hellenistic period The period of Greek and Middle Eastern history from the death of Alexander the Great in 323 BC to the Roman conquest of Egypt in 30 BC, marked by an increase in Greek cultural influence abroad.

hierarchical society A society in which some people enjoy higher rank and therefore more privileges than others.

hieroglyphic A system of writing that uses pictures to symbolize words.

Hieroglyphics were used in ancient Egypt, Mexico, and other places.

Hinduism The dominant religion and CULTURE of India since ancient times. It includes the worship of many gods and a belief in reincarnation (rebirth).

Hittites A people, probably from southeast Europe, who migrated into ANATOLIA about 2000 BC. They established an empire that extended into Syria and lasted until c.1200 BC.

hominid Any of the Hominidae family of primates (apes) to which modern humans and their immediate ancestors and related forms belong. They are distinguished by their ability to walk upright on two feet.

Homo erectus Meaning "upright man," the species name for a human ancestor that lived from 1.9 million years ago to 400,000 years ago.

Homo habilis "Handy man," the scientific name for a species of human ancestor that lived 2.4–1.9 million years ago. It was the first hominid that could make tools.

Homo sapiens Meaning "wise man," the species name for modern humans, who came into existence 400,000 years ago.

hunter–gatherers People who follow a way of life based on hunting wild animals, fishing, and gathering wild food plants.

Hyksos A people from the Middle East who invaded northern Egypt from 1640–1532 BC and established a capital at Avaris in the Delta.

Ice Age A period of global cooling that lasted from one million years ago to 10,000 years ago. Ice covered large areas of land and sea levels were considerably lower.

Iron Age The period of prehistory following the BRONZE AGE when iron became widely used for making weapons and tools. Iron SMELTING began between 1400 and 1200 BC in ANATOLIA and spread from there into the Middle East, Europe, Asia, and Africa. Iron was not introduced into the Americas until the arrival of Europeans.

irrigation The watering of crops by artificial means. In the ancient world, canals were built to carry water from rivers or wells to the fields.

Macedon A powerful kingdom of northern Greece. Its king Alexander the Great conquered the PERSIAN empire from 334–326 BC.

Mandate of Heaven A doctrine used by all Chinese rulers until 1911 to justify their power. It stated that rulers were appointed by the gods.

Mauryan A powerful dynasty that ruled most of India from 381-185 BC.

Medes A NOMADIC people from Central Asia who settled in northern Iran during the 9th century BC. Their kingdom of Media was conquered by the PERSIANS in 550 BC.

megalithic Describes any structure built of large stones. The term is used particularly of the NEOLITHIC tombs and stone circles of western Europe such as Stonehenge in England. Many pre-Columbian structures in America are megalithic.

Mesopotamia Meaning in Greek "the land between the rivers," it is the name given by historians to the dry but fertile region between the Tigris and Euphrates rivers in modern Iraq where the world's first cities developed about 4000 BC.

monarchy A form of government in which power is held by one hereditary ruler such as a king or emperor.

mythology A collection of ancient stories about gods and superhuman heroes that were made up to explain the origins of the world, its natural phenomena, and the social customs of a particular CULTURE.

Neanderthals An extinct form of early humans who lived in Europe during the ICE AGE. They made flint tools and buried their dead.

Neolithic Meaning "new stone age," it describes the period of Asian and European prehistory between c.9000 and 2000 BC when crops and animals were domesticated and early farming societies developed.

nomads People who move from one place to another in search of food or water as the seasons change.

Nubia A region on the river Nile in Africa, roughly equivalent to modern Sudan, which was the site of an early CIVILIZATION that had close links to ancient Egypt.

Olmecs Corn farmers living on the Gulf coast of southeast Mexico who developed the first CIVILIZATION of the Americas (1200–400 BC).

Paleoindian A name used by archeologists to describe the first humans to settle in the Americas, the ancestors of the Native Americans.

papyrus A species of reed that was used in ancient Egypt to make paper.

pastoralism Farming based on grazing domestic animals rather than growing crops. Because grazing animals need to be moved to fresh pastures, pastoral people are NOMADS or seminomads.

patricians Members of the ARISTOCRACY of Roman society, descended from the original SENATE.

Persians The ancient Iranians, an Indo-European people related to the MEDES. The empire created by the Persian king Cyrus II (c.559–53 BC) dominated the Middle East until it fell to Alexander the Great in 330 BC.

pharaoh The title given to the kings of Egypt. It comes from an Egyptian word meaning "great palace."

Phoenicians The people of the narrow coastal plain of Lebanon and Syria, who established a trading empire in the Mediterranean from about 1000–500 BC. They were important in developing the alphabet from which later Middle Eastern and European alphabets are descended.

pictograph A symbol or picture that stands for a word or group of words. HIEROGLYPHIC writing used a form of pictograph. Chinese writing is based entirely on pictographs.

plebeians The name given to the ordinary working people of Roman society, who were not slaves.

province A subdivision of an empire, from the Latin word *provincia*. Any area conquered by the Romans was ruled as a province under a Roman governor. In the PERSIAN empire, provinces were known as satrapies and their governors as satraps.

Ptolemaic The dynasty founded by the Greek general Ptolemy that ruled Egypt from 305 BC–30 BC. Its last ruler was the famous Cleopatra VII.

pyramid A building with a square base and four sloping triangular sides. Enormous stone pyramids were used as royal tombs in ancient Egypt.

Republic The word the Romans used for their state, in which officials were elected by the people.

Scythians A fierce NOMAD people who dominated the plains of Central Asia from about 700–300 BC. The western Scythians, living north of the Black Sea, traded with the Greeks.

Sea Peoples Invaders of Egypt in the 13th and 12th centuries BC, probably from the northern Aegean.

Seleucid The dynasty founded by the Greek general Seleucos that ruled the Middle East from 312 BC–64 BC.

Senate The ruling assembly of ancient Rome; originally the king's council. Under the REPUBLIC its members were appointed for life and advised officials such as the consuls.

Shang The first historical dynasty of ancient China. It ruled from about 1766–1122 BC.

smelting Extracting metal from mineral ores by heating them to very high temperatures.

sub-Saharan Africa The part of Africa south of the Sahara desert, which acts as a barrier dividing it from the coastal regions of North Africa.

Sumerians The people of Sumer, southern MESOPOTAMIA, who developed the world's first civilization from c.3400–2000 BC.

tribe A large social group comprising numerous families or CLANS united by ancestry, CULTURE, and territory.

tribune One of 10 representatives elected by the PLEBEIANS of ancient Rome to serve their interests.

tribute A payment, usually made in gold and silver but sometimes in people, by a conquered kingdom to the victor.

Trojan War A legendary war fought between the Greeks and the Trojans (the people of the city of Troy, on the coast of ANATOLIA).

tyrant In ancient Greece, a ruler who seized power unlawfully. Tyrants were not necessarily oppressive rulers— this association came later.

vassal A person or state that is subordinate or dependent on another.

Zealots Members of a Jewish sect who fought against Roman rule in Palestine around the time of Christ and were defeated at Masada.

Zhou The second and longest-ruling dynasty of China, which held power from 1122 BC–256 BC.

ziggurat In MESOPOTAMIA, a temple of rectangular tiers (large at the base, small at the top), linked by outside staircases and topped by a shrine.

FURTHER READING

GENERAL
Bahn, Paul G. (ed). *The Story of Archaeology*. New York: Weidenfeld and Nicolson, 1996.

Burell, Roy, and Connolly, Peter. *Oxford First Ancient History*. New York: Oxford University Press, 1997

de Blois, Lukas, and van der Spek, R. *An Introduction to the Ancient World*. New York: Routledge, 1997.

Fagan, Brian. *People of the Earth: an Introduction to World Prehistory*. 8th ed. Reading, MA: Addison-Wesley, 1995.

Fagan, Brian M., and Scarre, Christopher. *Ancient Civilizations*. Reading, MA: Addison-Wesley, 1996.

Haywood, John. *Ancient Civilizations of the Near East and Mediterranean*. New York: M.E. Sharpe, 1997.

Haywood, John et al. *Atlas of World History*. New York: M.E. Sharpe, 1997.

Johanson, Donald C. and Edgar, Blake. *From Lucy to Language*. New York: Simon and Schuster, 1996.

Robinson, Andrew. *The Story of Writing*. London: Thames and Hudson, 1995.

ANCIENT MESOPOTAMIA
Roaf, Michael. *Cultural Atlas of Mesopotamia and the Ancient Near East*. New York: Facts on File, 1990.

ANCIENT EGYPT
Davies, Vivian, and Friedman, Renée. *Egypt Uncovered*. New York: Stewart, Tabori, and Chang, 1998.

Freeman, Charles. *The Legacy of Ancient Egypt*. New York: Facts on File, 1997.

Reeves, C. N. *The Complete Tutankhamen*. New York: Thames and Hudson, 1995.

LANDS OF THE BIBLE
Conolly, Peter. *The Holy Land*. New York: Oxford University Press, 1999.

Harris, Roberta. *The World of the Bible*. New York: Thames and Hudson, 1995.

Rogerson, John. *Atlas of the Bible*. New York: Facts on File, 1985.

PREHISTORIC EUROPE
Cunliffe, Barry (ed). *Prehistoric Europe: An Illustrated History*. New York: Oxford University Press, 1997.

ANCIENT GREECE
Boardman, John, et al. *The Oxford History of the Classical World*. New York: Oxford University Press, 1986.

Conolly, Peter. *The Ancient Greece of Odysseus*. New York: Oxford University Press, 1999.

Hornblower, Simon and Spawforth, Anthony. *The Oxford Companion to Classical Civilization*. New York: Oxford University Press, 1998.

ALEXANDER THE GREAT & HIS SUCCESSORS
Walbank, F.W. *The Hellenistic World*. Cambridge, MA: Harvard University Press, 1993.

Wood, Michael, *In the Footsteps of Alexander the Great*. Berkeley, CA: University of California Press, 1998.

THE RISE OF ROME
Boardman, John, et al. *The Oxford History of the Classical World*. New York: Oxford University Press, 1986.

Cornell, Tim and Matthews, John. *Atlas of the Roman World*. New York: Facts on File, 1983.

Drinkwater, J.F., Drummond, Andrew, Freeman, Charles *World of the Romans*. New York: Oxford University Press, 1993.

Hornblower, Simon and Spawforth, Anthony. *The Oxford Companion to Classical Civilization*. New York: Oxford University Press, 1998.

EARLY STATES OF SOUTH ASIA
Allchin, Bridget and Raymond. *The Rise of Civilization in India and Pakistan*. Cambridge, MA: Cambridge University Press, 1982.

FIRST EMPERORS OF CHINA
Blunden, Caroline and Elvin, Mark. *Cultural Atlas of China*. 1983. New York: Facts on File, 1998.

Chang, Kwang-Chih. *The Archaeology of Ancient China*. New Haven, CT: Yale University Press, 1997.

INDEX

ACKNOWLEDGMENTS

Front cover & 1 Erich Lessing/AKG; **2–3** P. Koch/RHPL; **6** Erich Lessing/AKG; **10** Natural History Museum, London; **10–11** Hutchison Library; **13** AKG; **14–15 & 15** Erich Lessing/AKG; **17** WFA/Anthropology Museum, Veracruz University, Jalapa; **18–19** Robert McLeod/RHPL; **19** RHPL; **20** Erich Lessing/AKG; **21** B. Norman/Ancient Art & Architecture Collection Ltd; **22 & 23** Erich Lessing/AKG; **24–25** WFA; **25** Copyright British Museum; **26** WFA; **27** Copyright British Museum; **28t & 28b** Erich Lessing/AKG; **29** The Stock Market; **30** Erich Lessing/AKG; **31** The Stock Market; **33** Hanny Paul/Gamma/Frank Spooner Pictures; **34** John Haywood; **34–35, 35t, 35b, 36t & 36b** Erich Lessing/AKG; **38** John Haywood; **38–39** Erich Lessing/AKG; **40** John Haywood; **42 & 45** Erich Lessing/AKG; **46–47** Powerstock/Zefa Photo Library; **47** WFA/Private Collection; **48 & 50** Erich Lessing/AKG; **51** RHPL; **52** P. Koch/RHPL; **54** Adam Woolfitt/RHPL; **55** Ashmolean Museum, Oxford; **58** Tiziana & Gianni Baldizzone/Corbis; **59** RHPL.

Timetable background (5) 23, 27, 31, 35, 39, 43, 47, 51, 55 & 59
Babylonian plan of the world (detail): Michael Holford

Abbreviations

AKG Archiv für Kunst und Geschichte

RHPL Robert Harding Picture Library

WFA Werner Forman Archive

Artists

John Fuller, Charles Raymond, Roger Stewart, Andrew Wheatcroft

Every effort has been made to trace copyright holders of the pictures used in this book.
Anyone having claims to ownership not identified above is invited to contact Andromeda Oxford Limited.